How to Find
Almost Anyone,
Anywhere

How to Find Almost Anyone, Anywhere

Revised Edition

Norma Mott Tillman
Private Investigator

Rutledge Hill Press®

Nashville, Tennessee

Copyright © 1994, 1998 by Norma Mott Tillman.

Published in Nashville, Tennessee, by Rutledge Hill Press®, Inc., 211 Seventh Avenue North, Nashville, Tennessee 37219.
Distributed in Canada by H. B. Fenn & Company, Ltd., 34 Nixon Road, Bolton, Ontario L7E 1W2. Distributed in Australia by The Five Mile Press Pty., Ltd., 22 Summit Road, Noble Park, Victoria 3174. Distributed in New Zealand by Tandem Press, 2 Rugby Road, Birkenhead, Auckland 10. Distributed in the United Kingdom by Verulam Publishing, Ltd., 152a Park Street Lane, Park Street, St. Albans, Hertfordshire AL2 2AU.

Typography by Compass Communications, Inc., Nashville, Tennessee.
Design by Bruce Gore, Gore Studios, Nashville, Tennessee.

Library of Congress Cataloging-in-Publication Data

Tillman, Norma Mott, 1938–
　　How to find almost anyone, anywhere / Norma Mott Tillman.—Rev. ed.
　　　p.　cm.
　　Includes bibliographical references and index.
　　ISBN 1-55853-657-4
　　1. Missing persons—United States—Investigation. 2. Birthparents—United States—Identification.　I. Title.
　　HV6762.U5T55　1998　　　　　　　　　　　　　　　　98-30964
　　363.2'336—dc21　　　　　　　　　　　　　　　　　　　　CIP

Printed in the United States of America
1 2 3 4 5 6 7 8 9 — 02 01 00 99 98

How to Find
Almost Anyone,
Anywhere
Revised Edition

~

Acknowledgments

This book is dedicated to my sister Barbara Meroney and my friends Darlyn Farris and Shirley Crick. I have watched as all three of these people have followed in my footsteps and I'm very proud of what they have accomplished. Without their help I don't know how I would have been able to make this book possible. I am truly grateful for all their support and encouragement. I'm proud to pass the torch of being one of the leading missing persons experts on to my sister. Barbara has truly paid her dues and is one of the best.

I would also like to thank the individuals who helped with the updating of specific chapter: Lynn Ingram for the Adoption chapters; Neff Hudson for the Military chapter; Sheri Herold for the Deadbeat Dads chapter; and Barbara Renick for the Genealogy chapter. I extend my thanks to R. Scott Grasser for his valuable input for the Internet chapter and use of resources from his book, *FINDsomeone.com*. And a special thanks to Jack Richard for his permission to use selections from his article, "Ring That Bell . . .".

Contents

Preface   *ix*

1. Internet   1

2. Searching for the Seed to the Solution   7

3. Types of Missing Persons and Property   15

4. Starting Your Search   27

5. Gathering Information   35

6. From My Files: Real Searches for Real People   55

7. Finding Your Father   75

8. Looking for Your Mother   85

9. Adoption: The Decision of a Lifetime   91

10. Brothers, Sisters, and Long-Lost Cousins   119

11. Best Friends and First Loves   133

12. Men and Women in Uniform: Military Searches   141

13. The Buck Stops Here:
    Deadbeat Dads and Other People Who Owe Money   153

14. Tracing Your Family Tree   163

15. Reference Section   183

    Suggested Readings   236

Preface

DEAR NORMA

My parents divorced when I was only five years
old. My father was career military. I do not know why
they divorced, but my mother always told my brother
and me that if our father really cared about us he
would contact us, but he never did. I have always
wanted to find him, but my mother would not help. I
am now thirty-two years old, married, and the mother
of three children. I want my children to meet and
know their grandfather. It was very difficult growing
up without my father. We really loved him and
needed him.

I have tried writing the military records center
and have contacted the military locating service, but
no one will give me any information. I know my
father paid child support and that it was automatically deducted from his military paycheck, but the government will not give me anything. I asked them to
forward a letter to him, but the letter was returned. I
don't know where else to turn.
—SALLY

I am often asked, "What made you become a private investigator?" I did not plan it, but it seemed like the most natural

thing in the world for me to do because I am very independent, persistent, determined, intuitive, inquisitive, decisive, and innovative—qualities that are helpful to a private investigator.

What keeps me going are letters like the one on the previous page from people searching for their father, their child, a brother or sister, or a long-lost friend. Sally, who wrote this letter to me, had her father's full name, his date of birth, and his military I.D. number. With this much information it should be easy to find her father, but she did not know how. And the government was not going to help her. With the information I give in this book, however, finding her father would not be difficult.

Nothing has ever been dull, boring, or routine for me. Early on I was curious and adventurous, always exploring the world around me. Living on the edge has been my way of life since childhood, and mysteries have always fascinated me. As you might suspect, other children my age did not share my interests. In addition, I have always been independent, which allows me to do what I want to do, when I want to do it. Of course, because investigators spend so much time alone, on the road tracking down clues, this sense of independence has served me well.

I didn't appreciate the value of having two talented and creative parents until I was grown and had a family of my own. Nor did I realize how much they impacted and influenced my life as they helped to set me on a course. My father was a homicide detective who worked with the Nashville Police Department since before I was born. When he came home for dinner, I would sit in his car and listen to the police dispatcher. His homicide reference books fascinated me, and by the age of ten I was familiar with such terms as point of entry, decapitation, angle of attack, rape, homicide, death, and evidence. He was intuitive and had an analytical mind.

My mother was a gifted person who did not have any limits to her numerous talents. Every time I see a beautiful garden I am reminded of the beautiful flowers in our back yard that were my mother's pride and joy—second only to my two younger sisters and myself. My mother had eighty-five varieties of iris and kept an itemized record of the names of the flowers and the dates they bloomed.

I inherited many qualities from my parents (who died before seeing me become an investigator) that have contributed to my success as an investigator, and I attribute many of my skills—the ability to improvise, to find my way around a new place, and to survive in the outdoors—to the years I spent in Girl Scouts and in summer camps.

After graduating from high school, I skipped college and went to Washington to work for the federal government. When my mother died, I transferred back to Nashville and got a job with the Internal Revenue Service. A few years later I began working with the police department and studied criminal law. After eleven years of working in law enforcement, during which time I learned about shooting a gun, performing emergency medical training, criminal law, accident investigation, hostage negotiation, officer survival skills, and self-defense, I experienced burn out.

For the next two years I worked as an insurance fraud investigator and learned about civil law and civil investigations. Even though I had mastered the police department's data bases, I was not aware of the many public records that were available and the miles and miles of paper trails on almost all private citizens. During this time, several attorneys began asking me to find a missing witness, an heir to an estate, or someone else. I obtained a private investigator's license and learned what I needed to know to find information or people by trial and error. Fortunately, I had numerous contacts and knew my way around Nashville and how to work with the police department. Working as a private investigator began as only a sideline. Then as word got around, and as my reputation grew, I found myself doing full-time what I enjoyed most—finding information and locating missing people.

The ability to find missing persons is a special gift from God. I could never do this alone. I am grateful that He has allowed me to help numerous people find important people missing from their lives. Reuniting loved ones is one of the most rewarding experiences I have ever had. In order to help as many people as possible, I am sharing my knowledge, experience, and resources in this book. I sincerely hope that this information will help you to find the missing person in your life.

How to Find
Almost Anyone,
Anywhere
Revised Edition

1

Internet

∾

IN THE FEW SHORT YEARS since I revealed in *How to Find Almost Anyone, Anywhere* the secrets I had learned in finding more than 1,000 people, the availability of information to help find people has exploded due to the Internet. There are many books that specifically tell you about using the Internet to find missing loved ones, birth parents, friends, deadbeat dads, or others. One of the best resources for learning how to use the Internet to find people is *FINDsomeone.com* by R. Scott Grasser. This book can be found at your local bookstore or on the Web at www.amazon.com. The Internet's effect on searching has been most significant in genealogical searches and adoption searches because searchers in both these areas have formed support groups that communicate by using the Internet.

But although the Internet has revolutionized the way you get information, the principles in this book remain the same. The Internet may make it easier for you to find a phone number and address of a long lost brother or sister, but you still have to carefully plan how you will approach that person. That's where *How to Find Almost Anyone, Anywhere* comes in. It will tell you what information to look for and what to do with it once you have it. It will also tell you of the experiences of others who have gone through the same process you are going through.

The Internet is simply a way of getting information over the phone line (or through special cables) through your computer. The Internet is not the same thing as the World Wide Web, which is only one part of the Internet.

A Brief History

The Internet began in 1969 with a defense project to keep American military sites in communication with each other in the event of a nuclear war. Once the mainframes in these military sites were connected so that messages and a few files could be transferred, work was begun on connecting additional computers. During the 1970s, this was referred to as the Network Control Protocol. The term *Internet* was probably first used in 1973 and something similar to what we know today was first demonstrated in 1977. The development of Internet technology took about fourteen years and as late as 1983 was still used only by the military.

In 1984, the National Science Foundation (NSF) contracted with a non-profit corporation of Michigan Universities to build an electronic network. A number of other universities and research groups joined in, and by 1986 NSFNET was operational. A key difference between the two networks at the time was that the older military network excluded people and institutions that were not connected with the military while NSFNET's purpose seemed to be to connect as many people and institutions as it could.

By 1988, the online community, which by this time included a number of commercial services, suffered from "e-mail islands." If you wanted to send e-mail to someone on MCI Mail, you had to have an account at MCI Mail. If you wanted to send e-mail to CompuServe, you had to have an account on CompuServe. This was clearly a problem, therefore a group of defense contractors, led by Boeing, demanded that the various online services interconnect. Since interconnection was of such obvious benefit to e-mail users, once one commercial service offered interconnection, all services had to do so. Within 18 months everybody was offering it.

The World Wide Web was started in 1989 by Tim Berners-Lee at CERN in Switzerland to help researchers in high-energy particle physics share information. It used hypertexts, which contain links that, when chosen, cause other documents to be retrieved and displayed on the user's computer. In 1992, vice-president Al Gore proposed legislation, which was eventually passed, to fund a National Research and Education Network that would connect schools and libraries.

In 1993, a small group at the University of Illinois at Champaign/Urbana had developed an interface to the World Wide Web that they called Mosaic. This browser allows users to navigate the Web by using their mouse to click on links. More importantly, however, the browser was extensible, allowing users to add sound, video clips, or almost anything. Today variations of Mosaic still are the key to using the Web easily.

On April 30, 1995, the National Science Foundation Network's backbone of the Internet ceased operations. No longer did the NSF provide a place for computers to connect. In its place are four Network Access Points (NAPs), which are operated by private companies. They are Pacific Bell in San Francisco, Ameritech Advanced Data Services and Bellcore in Chicago, Sprint in New York, and Metropolitan Fiber Systems in Washington, D.C. The Internet is simply the telephone links to one of these NAPs. If you live six blocks from the nearest person linked to the Internet, when you hook up, you have just expanded the Internet by six blocks.

The use of the Internet and the World Wide Web is exploding and will continue to change the way we communicate and find information. This makes finding people easier because searching for people requires information and information is much more easily available on the Internet than it ever was before.

Using the World Wide Web

If you have no experience in "surfing the Web," you can master the basics in just a few minutes at your local library. Most libraries have computers available for general use that have access to the Web. There are thousands of resources available to you on the Web, and I will mention some of them in the following chapters. Here I want to mention a few of the more general ones.

The most obvious resources on the Web are telephone and e-mail directories. These are usually a long shot for finding someone because the person must be listed and you need to know the city where the person lives. The National Credit Information (NCI) is a professional on-line searchable database found at www.reunion.com. It contains over 3 billion records including names, birthdates, Social Security numbers, addresses, vehicle registration, and voter registration. Professional databases charge a fee for their service. The Internet Sleuth (www. isleuth.com) lists more than 3,000 data banks and contains a reverse white pages. Here is a list of some of the data banks with e-mail directories, toll free directories, yellow page (business) directories, and white page (residential) directories. More Websites are listed in the Reference Chapter on page 190.

E-mail Directories
- FOUR11 DIRECTORIES www.four11.com
- INFOPLUS INTERNET DIRECTORY
  www.infop.com/phone/isearch.html

Toll-free Directories
- AT&T 800 DIRECTORY att.net/dir800/
- INTERNET 800 DIRECTORY   inter800.com/

White Pages Directories
- 555-1212   www.555-1212.com/
- WHOWHERE PHONE DIRECTORY
  www.whowhere.com/phone.html

- SWITCHBOARD www.switchboard.com
- YAHOO PEOPLE SEARCH
  www.yahoo.com/search/people/

Yellow Pages Directories

- AMERICAN BUSINESS
  INFORMATION-LOOKUP www.lookupusa.com/
- GTE SUPER PAGES
  INTERACTIVE SERVICE   superpages.gte.com/
- YELLOW PAGES ON LINE   www.ypo.com/
- CANADA 411   canada411.sympatico.ca

Links to Information Sites of Interest www.reunion.com

Websites generally fall into two categories: commercial sites operated by companies or private individuals; and public sites operated by the government, educational institutions, and non-profit associations. You can tell the difference between the two simply by looking at their Web address. If it ends in .gov (government), .com (commercial), or .net (network), the site is a commercial entity. If it ends in .mil (military), .edu (education), or .org (organization), it is a public site that does not attempt to make a profit.

The distinction is important for assessing the accuracy of the information on the site. Some commercial sites are nothing more than one person's opinion. But others are run by information brokers or newspapers with years of experience in processing and distributing data. A similar logic applies to public sites. The government offers a wealth of free information, but it shies away from releasing anything it considers sensitive. Some government agencies are making their records (or contents of their records) available on the Internet. Because of the privacy laws, however, most government records cannot be retrieved without a written and signed request. The government Websites usually have forms for requesting records that can be downloaded and printed out. Associations tend to owe their existence to a cause, so they might not be completely objective. The most important thing to remember is that not everything published on the Internet is true, unbiased, or even valuable.

Here are some helpful Websites that provide some immediate information.

- SOCIAL SECURITY DEATH INDEX
  www.ancestry.com/ssdi
- LANDINGS (aircraft registration) www1.drive.net
- COPYRIGHT REGISTRATION SEARCH
  marvel.loc.gov
- US POSTAL SERVICE ZIP+4   www.usps.gov/ncsc
- DOCTOR SEARCH DATABASE
  www.ama-assn.org/

Another important resource on the Internet is the many newsgroups on a variety of topics. Newsgroup search (www.dejanews.com) provides lists of newsgroups. Service providers, such as AOL, also provide access to newsgroups.

A newsgroup is a place where individuals can post messages or information for others to read. Just as the phone directories are a long shot for finding someone, when searching through newsgroups, you rely on the chance that someone reading your message will know where the person is for whom you are looking. But it is a free service and may be beneficial. Someone may, however, provide you with information that could open new doors in your search. Most importantly, newsgroups allow you to speak (via messages) with other people in the same situation as yourself, blow off some steam when you get frustrated, and learn how to get around dead ends.

2

Searching for the Seed
to the Solution

Dear Norma,

I am forty-two years old and have never met my father. I am happily married and the mother of two grown children.

My mother is now deceased, but before her death she revealed the name of my real father, Edward Stevenson. She would never discuss this with me although I asked her for information when I was sixteen and learned that the name of the man on my birth certificate was not my real father.

During the war, in 1943, my mother worked at a plant in Ohio. A co-worker named Edward Stevenson took my mother out one night. They went to a local bar and had a few drinks, then went for a drive. I was conceived that night. By the time my mother found out she was pregnant, she had discovered Edward Stevenson was married. She was ashamed, embarrassed, and humiliated. She felt cheap and dirty. She could not tell anyone. Instead, she quit her job and moved away. She never told Edward Stevenson that he had fathered her child.

Her high-school sweetheart came home from overseas and they got married when she was two months pregnant. She did not tell him she was pregnant. He left and went back overseas. When I was born, she put his name as the father on my birth certificate. Of course, he found out about me and knew I was not his child and he divorced my mother. At least that made it appear to everyone that my mother was divorced, not an unwed mother. She never told anyone her secret.

At age sixteen, I wanted to meet my father. At that time, my mother had to admit to me that the man listed on my birth certificate was not my father. At that time, she refused to give me any other information. One day, as my mother lay dying, she told me that my biological father's name was Edward Stevenson and that he was very handsome—6'5" tall, with dark hair and dark eyes. He was a supervisor at the plant and a Union representative. She did not tell me much more. By this time, her speech and memory were failing. She died soon after telling me my father's name. I did not have much to work with.

After my mother's death, I asked her sister if she knew who my father was. She told me she thought he was from New Jersey. I wrote to the New Jersey Office of Vital Statistics for a birth certificate for Edward Stevenson. Because I did not have his age or date of birth, I asked them to search for all persons with that name born from 1900 to 1930. They sent me a copy of a 1911 birth certificate with the name I was looking for. For the next two years, I searched for the man on the birth certificate. I even went to New Jersey myself. I spent several thousand dollars and several years searching for my father, without success.

I want to assure you—and him—that I seek only information. I do not want to cause him problems or embarrassment. I need my medical history as well as other genealogical information pertaining to my heritage. I want to know all I can about this man, but I do not expect a relationship, nor do I want anything from him. He need not fear me, because I do not mean any harm.

Please help make my life complete. Help me find my father.

—JAN

≈ ≈ ≈

Dear Jan,

Based on the information you furnished, I too thought New Jersey would be the logical place to begin. After going to New Jersey and verifying the information you were given, I discovered that the birth certificate you were given was in error. The child whose certificate you were given was actually the child's father. The name of that child's father had mistakenly been entered in the space provided for the child's name. Because the child's name was entirely different, I realized the man you had been searching for was not the right person. Once I discovered this mistake, the obvious place to begin the search was at the plant in Ohio.

Unfortunately, the plant had been closed for years, so how could I find anyone to ask? I decided to begin at the local public library. I went to the reference section to look for 1943 directories. There was a city directory for that year, which contained the names of two men with the same name as your father. One of the names appeared in the current city directory. I drove to the address listed in the directory and talked to a man named Edward Stevenson. He was not the

right one. I asked him if he happened to know the
whereabouts of the other man and he responded, "I
heard he lived in Alabama." I thanked him and gave
him my name and phone number, in case he wanted
to contact me in the future with additional information. (Norma's Note: Always leave your name and
phone number so that you may be contacted easily.)

After returning home, I received a phone call
from Edward Stevenson of Ohio. He remembered
that the other Edward Stevenson had moved to
Tuscaloosa, Alabama.

All I had to do was ask directory assistance in
Tuscaloosa, Alabama, for a number for Edward
Stevenson. I dialed the number and a man answered.
My heart was pounding.

"Is this Edward Stevenson?"

"Yes," he said.

"Are you by any chance the same Edward
Stevenson who worked at the Bridge plant in
Cincinnati, Ohio, in 1943?"

"Yes, I am."

"Were you 6'5", with dark curly hair and were you
a Union representative?"

"Yes."

"Mr. Stevenson, may I speak to you about something very personal, very confidential? If this is not a
convenient time, I will be glad to give you my phone
number and you may call me back, or I can call you
back."

"Honey, you go right ahead and ask me anything
you want to."

"Do you happen to remember a co-worker named
Jane Vaughan?"

"No, I don't believe I do. That was a long time ago."

"Well, Mr. Stevenson, to make a long story short,

Jane Vaughan became pregnant by a co-worker
named Edward Stevenson. She never told Mr.
Stevenson about their daughter."

Dead silence! Then a voice said, "It wasn't my
husband; he was married to me then." His wife had
been listening the entire time. She took over and did
all the talking, convincing me I had made a big mistake. She told me of another man named Edward
Stevenson who also worked at the plant. Of course, I
had already visited the other one, who was 5'10",
with green eyes and red hair.

I knew I had the right one, I just didn't want to
hurt anyone, so I said, "I'm so sorry, I must have made
a mistake. I didn't mean to cause anyone a problem."
Mr. Stevenson was still on the line, even though he
did not say a word. After Mrs. Stevenson hung up, he
said, "Would you send me her picture?"

"The mother or the daughter?" I asked.

"Both," he responded. I asked him where he wanted me to send them and he gave me his home address.

"Are you sure?" I asked.

"Yes," he said.

—NORMA

*I contacted Jan and she wrote her father a letter and sent pictures of
her family. Mrs. Stevenson wrote Jan back and said, "What do you
want? Leave my husband alone. Do not contact him again, he is not
well." Later Jan learned that Mr. Stevenson confessed to his wife
that he had been unfaithful.*

*Of course, Jan was devastated by Mrs. Stevenson's letter. She
did not want anything except to meet her father. She wrote back,
begging for a few minutes of his time so that they might actually meet
one another. Finally, Mrs. Stevenson wrote that Jan and her husband could meet the Stevensons in Little Rock. She insisted that Jan
could spend fifteen minutes with Mr. Stevenson. During their meet-*

ing, Mrs. Stevenson did all the talking. Jan brought pictures of her son and daughter. Her son was 6'5", with dark, wavy hair—the very image of Mr. Stevenson. At last, Jan met her father. He was distant, but Jan can live with what she learned. Until she met him, she had to imagine what he was like. Now she knew. And for her, the search had been about information, not a relationship.

You've picked up this book because you want to find someone or find out information about somebody. Perhaps you were separated from your father or mother. Perhaps you gave up a child for adoption. Perhaps you've become romantically involved with a person and want to know something about his or her past before you continue the relationship.

Every person who has lost track of a parent, brother, sister, or other loved one has a void inside that aches with fear, longing, curiosity, and sometimes guilt. This is particularly true when family members are separated from each other by adoption or divorce. But it can also happen to men and women who have lost friends, first loves, or military buddies.

Many people doubt that they can actually find the person or information they want. Let me assure you that in reality, it's not hard to do. It just takes persistence and ingenuity.

Over the past few years, I've located more than one thousand missing persons and I orchestrate more than one hundred televised reunions per year between loved ones who have been separated. I've looked for many kinds of people and information. Your search will take hard work, but I can guarantee you that success is almost always possible.

Understand that most missing persons are not actually missing. They just don't know that anyone is looking for them. Therefore, unless someone is missing because of foul play, deliberate evasion, or participation in a witness protection program, he or she probably can be found. The average American will leave a paper trail seven miles long during a lifetime: credit cards, driver's license, automobile registration, medical records, insurance policies, marriage license(s), divorce and bankruptcy proceedings, bank accounts, and more. In Chapter Five, I list forty-three different records that usually exist on the average American.

As you look for those records on the person you are trying to find, most may lead to dead ends. But you only need one live one. Remember that every problem has a seed to the solution. You just need to find it.

For one person, it may be only an old automobile registration. But that can give you an address where the person you are trying to find used to live. And the landlord might have some information. For another person, it may be a place of employment. You may find only one record on your person, but it can lead to the information you need.

The four pieces of information that will help you most in your search are the person's name, date of birth, Social Security number, and last known address. With these four pieces of information, you will almost be guaranteed success in locating a missing person.

As you read through this book, I'm going to let you take a peek at some of my correspondence. Some of the letters include my answers to the writers; others leave the solution to you and your imagination. I've disguised names and locations, but I think you'll soon realize that if you're searching for someone, you aren't alone.

No matter who (or what) you're searching for, all searches have common threads. For that reason, you'll probably see that, at times, I've repeated some information in the pages that follow. You'll want to read chapters that aren't necessarily about your specific search, because there may be something helpful in them.

For example, searches for fathers and for mothers are similar in many ways as long as you begin with a correct name. And a search for an adoptee is closely related to biological mother and father searches because of one common denominator: the adoption process. It would be wise for you to read all the chapters and to take note of any relevant information, no matter where you find it.

The final chapter of the book contains lists of information, Websites, addresses, e-mail addresses, phone numbers, sample forms, and other information that will be helpful to you. Be sure to check it out—you may find just what you need to locate the seed to your solution. That seed, or piece of information, will allow you to write or call public agencies, access Websites that will allow you to research city directories and telephone books, ask revealing questions, and access databases until you find the contact information you need.

Once you've read this book, the best advice I can give you is to start with what you know, and follow it until you've solved your personal mystery.

And let me make one more point before we get started. I am a firm believer in keeping the law. After eleven years of experience with law enforcement, I have a healthy respect for law and order. Remember: You do not have to break the law to find a missing person. I don't break the law in my searches, and I don't want you to either. So if you're interested in wiretaps, breaking and entering, trespassing, or getting information through bribery or other covert means, this isn't the book for you. Instead, this is a book for real people with a real need for a reunion.

> *Every problem contains the seed for the solution.*
> *Your goal is to find the seed in your search.*

3

Types of Missing Persons and Property

A MISSING PERSON is simply a person whom the searcher cannot find. Most missing persons are actually not missing at all; they simply don't know anyone is looking for them.

There are two basic categories of missing persons: criminal and noncriminal. These two basic categories also can be referred to as voluntary and nonvoluntary.

To find almost anyone, whether criminal or noncriminal, the search must have a starting point. Whatever information you have to work with is your starting point. Your mission is to follow "clues" or "trails" that branch from your starting point.

Although I hate to admit it, there are some missing persons that classify as impossible searches. It is almost impossible to find information on a person if you don't have a correct name. Persons who were abandoned have no paper trails. Therefore without a trail, there is nothing to follow. Persons who disappeared due to foul play may not be located if no body is found. Children are difficult to locate because frequently no paper trail exists. The only information to work with is furnished by a witness or person who knew something of the disappearance. And it may be impossible to find a person whose records have been falsified.

Types of Missing Persons and Property

Abandoned Money and Unclaimed Property

Several agencies of the federal government, as well as every state, hold abandoned money until someone comes forward to claim it. A list of national and state unclaimed property offices can be found in the Reference Section.

Most unclaimed property results when an owner dies and no heirs or beneficiaries collect it. This property can be a bank account, an insurance policy, real estate, a will, or other assets. After seven years, this property is transferred to a state Office of Unclaimed Property and it is held there until the rightful owner claims it. Because most people don't know they have anything waiting for them, they never inquire.

Lists of unclaimed properties are available in every state. Most states allow a "finder's fee" for anyone who locates an heir to unclaimed property. Finder's fees vary by state, anywhere from 10 percent of the amount of the property to an unlimited amount. The problem with collecting a finder's fee is that you must do all the work at your own expense, find the people, and then try to get them to sign a contract authorizing you to receive a percentage. There is no guarantee you will collect a dime. This is a risk you may not want to take. (If you are curious to know if you are an heir, you may want to consult a professional heir finder.)

For unclaimed property to be claimed, absolute proof of identity and ownership is necessary. Each state provides forms to be completed by both the finder and the next of kin.

For a small research fee you may write to see if you or a relative has unclaimed stock certificates:

Stock Search International
4761 West Waterbuck Drive
Tuscon, AZ 85742
(800) 537-4523
e-mail: ssi@stocksearchintl.com
Website: www.stocksearchintl.com

Adoption

I believe the adoption search is the most difficult search of all. Few clues usually exist and most states have closed records, leaving the searcher few trails to follow.

According to the *Congressional Record*, there are an estimated five million adoptees in the United States, and two million adoptees are actively searching for biological families every day. Counting the biological parents, siblings, grandparents, aunts and uncles, and other relatives, it is estimated that approximately 135 million people have been involved in the adoption process.

Adoption searches, like other kinds of searches, must begin with whatever information is known about the person being sought. If the searcher is an adoptee, the search for the birth parents may begin with the medical records at birth. If the searcher is the birth parent, the record may begin with a search of records at a courthouse.

There are many Websites available to help you in adoption searches. There are Websites that provide information about local adoption laws and the process for obtaining information. There are also many support groups, which can be accessed on the Web, that can offer help in your search.

The adoption search is more involved than any other search because the search itself is only part of the process. Both the searcher and the missing person will need to be prepared for their reunion. The approach to the missing person is extremely delicate. An inexperienced searcher could ruin a person's life if he or she does not understand the importance of the approach and the preparation required. Adoption searches can be very successful, and happy reunions are possible as long as there is a good understanding of the adoption process.

Ancestors

A genealogical search for ancestors can begin with whatever information you know about yourself. If you know who your parents were and where they were born, it is possible to search through libraries, family Bibles, cemetery records, census records, immigration records, and church records.

One of the largest depositories for genealogical records is the Mormon libraries, with branches in every state. These libraries, whose records are primarily more than fifty years old, can be accessed on-line. In addition, the National Archives has regional libraries and may conduct a search for you by written request.

Census records are maintained on microfilm and are released after the records are seventy years old. The records are released in ten-year increments. The last available census is the 1920 census. Most reference sections of public libraries have these records. To search them, you must understand Soundex, a coding system in which vowels and consonants are assigned a numerical code number. If the name you are searching can be spelled several ways, this coding system will allow you to view all possible names. Once you locate the name you are searching for, the census will give you the names and ages of all persons in that household for that year.

Records exist in book form of passenger lists of persons arriving in this country. These lists will also contain the number of persons in this family, which port they entered, which state and county they settled in, and other information. This information may be requested in writing for a fee, from branches of the National Archives libraries. Other public libraries may have this information in their reference sections. Also be aware that each state has an archives library. These libraries are valuable sources of information and have Web pages that can be accessed on the Internet. Reference librarians are usually very informative regarding material that may be researched. Within each state may be found a historical society or an agency for historical record keeping. Affiliates of these organizations might be able to assist you with your search.

There is also a wealth of information available on the World Wide Web regarding genealogical searches. There are special

Websites that allow you to search their databases for free, and others that let you post queries on the Internet. Of all the different types of searches, the genealogical search has the most resources available on the Internet.

Criminals

A criminal type of missing person is one who has committed a crime and is wanted by law enforcement. This person knows he or she is wanted and probably fears landing in jail. Even though a criminal is hiding or running, that person must continue daily life—eating, sleeping, surviving. All these activities have the potential to provide you with clues.

Criminals may go to great extremes to hide their whereabouts and will leave few, if any, paper trails. The criminal may even change identity either by using the identity of another person or by changing his or her own identity by transposing numbers in a Social Security number or using an incorrect birthdate. Identifying information is often false. The only paper trail criminals may leave may be their criminal history. However, in the attempt to survive, the criminal might have a vehicle, a driver's license, a Social Security number, a family, a job, insurance, bank accounts, and relatives and friends. A criminal may get sick, need to see a doctor or dentist, attend sports games, subscribe to magazines, and buy medicine. Each of these leaves a paper trail.

Criminals may have a pattern or "m.o."—method of operation or *modus operandi*. They are basically creatures of habit. By analyzing their m.o., you can almost predict their actions. The criminal mind is not complicated; it is just on a different track than the noncriminal's. In order to catch a criminal, you must be able to think like one. You have to figure out what you would do if you were in the same situation. The most difficult part of living a criminal life is not having any contact with your family or friends. Most criminals will eventually get in touch with someone they have known. The easiest way to locate a criminal is to find out who he or she is most likely to contact. It may take a while, but it will probably pay off.

On one criminal case I was able to make friends with the mail carrier of the criminal's parents and found out from what locations the person's parents received mail. On another case, I met the criminal's former girlfriend, who opened up to me and told me what I wanted to know. Finding a former spouse or former girlfriend/boyfriend can be one of the best sources of information about criminals.

With ex-cons, I have received information from a parole officer, a jail guard, and a bondsman. Anyone involved in the process of an arrest can provide information of some type. The criminal court clerk's office may have a copy of a warrant. An arrest record may reveal an attorney.

Because most criminals have a *history* of crime, you will want to analyze previous arrests. How about a bondsman? Who put up the money? By finding out who paid the bond and what the collateral was (maybe a piece of property, which would lead you to the property owner, which might lead you to the person you are looking for), you can find additional information that may lead to the whereabouts of your criminal. By finding out who visited the criminal while he or she was incarcerated, you will have some contacts. Just because they are criminals does not mean there is not a trail. The trail is different and difficult, but it is there.

Divorce

About 50 percent of all children in the United States are reared by single parents, primarily the mother. The absent parent may owe child support or, in the case of a man, may not even know he fathered a child. Probably the most requested search for a noncriminal type of missing person is the request to find a father.

If the parents are divorced, the divorce record is very important. In some states a divorce record will reveal the full names, dates of birth, Social Security numbers, and last known addresses of the parties involved. Also included on the divorce record may be an employer, a place of birth, a list of property, a disposition, and an attorney who represented each party.

For the person who is searching for a parent who was divorced, the first step is to obtain a copy of the divorce record.

Heirs/Beneficiaries

Heirs are persons to whom an estate has been left after a death. An heir to unclaimed property may not be aware of the estate. It takes at least nine months for an estate to be probated after a person's death. Once all debts are paid, if there is no will, the estate is divided among living heirs. If the next of kin is dead, the estate may be handed down to the survivors, who may not be aware of it.

Every state has an Office of Unclaimed Property. This office takes care of unclaimed property such as estates, insurance policies, and bank accounts until the proper owner, an heir or beneficiary, claims it.

The unclaimed property may not be turned over to the state until after seven years because, in the case of a bank or insurance policy, the executor of the estate must make every effort to locate and contact the heir. After all efforts have failed, the estate is then turned over to the state to be held in trust for the owner. States do not have on-staff investigators assigned to find these persons. Therefore almost anyone can conduct these types of searches, and most states do not require licensing. It may be fun to search for other people's heirs, but the risk of doing it without getting paid was discussed in the section in this chapter labeled "Abandoned Money and Unclaimed Property." Start by checking the laws in your state.

Persons who are heirs or beneficiaries probably do not know anyone is looking for them. They may not know they are due money or property. The searcher often does not have much to start with other than a name, and usually only the name of the deceased party. The deceased may have died several generations back and left his estate to a sibling or a sibling's children. By the time the searcher begins, perhaps fifty years have passed. The person's sibling may be deceased and have left seven children. The seven children may be deceased and have left thirty grandchildren. Now the searcher must find the thirty grandchildren. Heir searching may be time-consuming and costly, with no guarantee of any repayment of expenses.

Homeless

A homeless person may be classified as a noncriminal type of missing person. However, a homeless person may not leave a paper trail because he or she may not work, pay taxes, own a vehicle, possess a driver's license, or draw a paycheck. A homeless person may draw a welfare check, an unemployment check, food stamps, or receive Medicaid. Most homeless people will have a Social Security number even if they do not use it.

Many homeless people have been released from mental institutions. Some homeless persons have families they choose not to contact. And some homeless people choose this way of life.

A homeless person will probably have a birth certificate and a Social Security number. If the homeless person stays at a Salvation Army facility, a record may exist. The Salvation Army maintains a computer list of persons who stay at or are otherwise in contact with its many locations. Of course, the homeless person may not use his or her true identity. Therefore, any records that exist may not be 100 percent accurate. For information, contact:

> Salvation Army Social Services Dept.
> Missing Persons Bureau
> 440 West Nyack Road
> West Nyack, NY 10994-1739

It is possible for homeless people to sell or trade their identities. Birth certificates and Social Security numbers may be illegally sold. If the missing person does not work, pay taxes, draw a paycheck, have a bank account, or otherwise leave a paper trail, it will be very difficult to find him or her.

Military

Military searches can be difficult if the searcher is not the next of kin. If the searcher is a relative, there is a slim chance that writing to the National Personnel Records Center in St. Louis, Missouri, will provide information on the missing person. If the person is active military, there are military locating services available. If the person is inactive, there are many organizations that may be contacted. The Veterans' Administration (VA) has regional offices in which a searcher may inquire if the missing person has ever filed a claim for benefits. If a claim such as medical, retirement, disability, or death exists, the VA will verify the claim and provide the claim number. Depending on the year the claim was filed, the claim number may represent either the service I.D. number or the Social Security number.

The World Wide Web can be beneficial to military searches, although not as in-depth as for adoption or genealogical searches. There are Websites that offer the necessary forms for requesting information from various departments. There are also on-line military registries helping to being people together and publications that allow you to use their databases.

New Identity

To be truly undiscoverable, a person must change both internally (patterns and survival techniques) and externally (appearance).

To issue a Social Security card, a local Social Security office requires only a minimum level of proof that you are who you say you are, and that you were either born in the United States or are here lawfully. If the evidence you present looks good to the individual helping you, a card will be issued. Recently, it has become more difficult to obtain a card if you are over eighteen, because you have to have a good reason for not having needed a card earlier. The Social Security office is on guard for adults applying for cards. I understand that obtaining a card for a child is not questioned and can be done through the mail. If the child is deceased, the Social Security office may not even know. Once the card is issued, no one really checks to see the age of the person the card was issued to. Therefore anyone could possibly use the card on a very limited basis, without getting caught. Social Security does not perform a background check to confirm information.

An interesting observation is that the law only requires you to have a Social Security number to work and receive income in the United States. You are not required to use this number on any other document other than revenue-producing documents (Privacy Act of 1974). Voluntarily giving your Social Security number on medical forms, on insurance forms, and for credit purposes is unnecessary.

The person who has created a new identity will leave a trail, usually a false one, including credit cards and hotel records. Perhaps the most difficult aspect of creating a new identity is to sever all ties with the past. The past is the one link that can catch up with someone who does not wish to be found. Contact with a relative, friend, or associate; continuing a habit, hobby, or recreational pursuit; frequenting a business establishment; being on a mailing list; or following a pattern of any kind can cause someone who is hiding to be located. This is the ultimate game of "hide and seek."

Relatives

To find information about a missing family member, it may be necessary to talk to older family members. Try to talk with anyone who might have researched the family tree, because chances are that person will have already searched libraries, newspapers, and other reference sources.

Social Security records are confidential and not available for public or even law enforcement review. In some instances, the

Social Security office may provide certain limited information to the next of kin. Usually the office will verify whether a death claim is on file. On occasion, the Social Security office will forward a letter to the next of kin. The searcher will not receive any information. However, the letter will be returned if the person did not receive it. Therefore it is worth the effort to try this method.

The Internal Revenue Service also maintains an Office of Disclosure, which will forward a letter to the next of kin if the next of kin has filed an income tax return. Again, if the letter is returned to the sender, it never reached the intended party.

Runaways

A runaway can be classified as a noncriminal type of missing person. However, a runaway is probably hiding from a certain individual. Therefore a runaway may go to extremes not to leave a paper trail. In many instances a runaway is running from a very unhappy situation. A runaway may possess a driver's license and have a Social Security number. A young runaway may not have anything but a birth certificate. Usually, runaways become street survivors.

Witnesses

Attorneys need to locate witnesses to accidents as well as for other litigation purposes, both civil and criminal. Often the case is several years old by the time the attorney needs to actually depose or subpoena the witness, and by then the witness may no longer reside at the address given on the original report. Because of the time periods involved, it is not unusual for witnesses to move, which can make them extremely difficult to locate. A witness who is wanted only for a civil action lawsuit may be hiding from bill collectors and may not leave many trails, not even a forwarding address when moving.

Starting Your Search

REGARDLESS OF the type of search you are conducting, there is almost always a way to follow a trail of information. The beginning of the trail is the factual information you know about the person you are trying to find.

Profile the person you are searching for. Is the person missing because of: marital problems; financial problems; medical problems; career problems; or criminal problems? Does it appear the person is missing voluntarily or involuntarily? Is the missing person a criminal or noncriminal?

It is best to begin a search with a correct full name. However, many times searchers do not know the name of the person they seek. If you do not have a correct name to begin with, your first objective is to find the name.

The most important pieces of information needed to find almost anyone are: correct full name; date of birth; Social Security number; and last known address.

Write down the answers to these questions: Who am I searching for? Do I have a correct full name? If not, what do I know about this person? Where can I find this person's date of birth? Do I know where this person was born or do I have a last known address?

By using the sample checklists found in Chapter Fifteen, take a few minutes to write down whatever you do know about the person you want to find, where you need to go, and what you need to do. Don't weed out anything at this point. By making these checklists first, you will have specific goals to maintain and you will not waste valuable time or money.

Before you begin your search, spend some time searching the Web. Find out where to search, what forms you may need, and perhaps you may find the person you are looking for through one of the many databases available on the Web. You may also obtain valuable information from people through specific newsgroups where someone just might have answers regarding your search. No matter how much valuable information you get from the Web, eventually you will have to do some leg work. Before you leave home, refer to your checklists and make any necessary notes, such as directions to a building or office. If you are not familiar with the city in which you are searching, obtain a good street map. Always be prepared. Have plenty of change for parking meters, photocopy machines, and other incidentals. Carry a pen and paper at all times. Get in the habit of writing down everything you learn and experience, including dates, times, locations, phone numbers, people's names, and conversations.

Assuming you have a correct full name, is this last name (surname) a common or uncommon spelling? Believe it or not, the more uncommon a name is, the easier it is to find. Understand that many people change the spelling of their last name. A name may change an "i" to "y" or drop an "e." There may be many variations of the name over the decades. It is not unusual to find brothers who spell their last names differently, maybe by dropping a double letter or changing a vowel. Realize that women may be harder to locate than men because they are likely to change their names through marriage.

What if the person is hiding deliberately? Depending on why someone is missing, the person may deliberately change his or her name, either by switching the middle name and the first name, or by using a misspelled version. Someone who is running from the law or from bill collectors may try to throw off the pursuers in a number of ways.

It is difficult to exist in our society without leaving a paper trail. Even though a person may be hiding, he or she must have the basic necessities of food, clothing, and shelter. It is likely that the person will also have some form of transportation. But is anything on paper in his or her name? How about a telephone? Is the person on a mailing list?

Most people will have some form of identification, even if it is not authentic. Maybe it's a driver's license. Perhaps the person has health, life, or automobile insurance. Don't missing people get sick, need medicine, file medical claims? Missing people (criminals and noncriminals alike) may work, have hobbies and recreational interests, take vacations, and do almost anything the rest of us do.

If someone owes a lot of back child support or has a lot of bad debts and is wanted in order to be served with civil process, that person is going to take precautions to avoid being located. But it's doubtful that all family ties can be broken completely. A sister may receive a check and cash or deposit it for the person who is hiding. A relative may be helping the person hide.

Try to imagine what the person you are searching for must do with his or her time. Is he employed? Does he have hobbies? How does he spend his time? Does he have relatives? Does he visit them on holidays? Does he pay bills? If so, how? Does he buy food and other supplies? Does she have a car? Does she go to a dentist or doctor? Is she ever sick? Does he take prescription medicine? How does he pay for it? Is she drawing some type of unemployment check, disability, aid to dependent families, or other type of welfare?

No matter why someone is missing, there are certain basic needs that must be met. Your challenge is to determine what some of those needs might be and to try to follow the clues that those needs will produce.

If you do not have a correct full name, perhaps you know a city or state in which your missing person may have lived or where the individual was born. If you know a city or state, do you know the year your missing person resided there? If not, can you estimate the time? If so, what schools existed then? This is the way a trail begins, with whatever information you have at your fingertips or can obtain easily. Think about what the person might have been doing at a certain time. School? Work? A church, club, or organization? What relevant directories might exist? Is there a family cemetery? Are former neighbors still in the old neighborhood? Does the same mail carrier deliver the mail?

> *During a lifetime, the average American will leave a paper trail that extends approximately seven miles long.*

It is important to write down each "clue" because once you begin searching, each piece of information—no matter how insignificant it may seem at the time—may represent an important step in locating your missing person. Imagine that each clue is a piece of a puzzle, and as you find new clues you find new pieces. Little by little you finally have a complete picture—you locate your missing person.

Start with a notebook in which pages may be inserted. As you continue looking, you will locate various documents that relate to your search. Put your checklists in the front of the notebook for easy access.

As you search through information, remember that every state and every jurisdiction may have different ways of recording information, different laws, and different names of courts.

Be prepared to ask effective questions, and act confident

when you ask them. Look neat and professional in appearance, and don't overdress or underdress. Don't be offensive in your approach, and remain nonthreatening. No matter where you go or with whom you speak, probably the most important quality you can possess is a good attitude. Be cheerful, confident, and positive when conducting your investigation. Most of all, believe in yourself, and believe in your search.

Basic Investigative Techniques

In most cases of looking for someone, the searcher will have some information to begin with. By listing each fact or rumor you have heard, along with the name of the person you heard this from, you can begin an information log. This log is merely a way of keeping up with information in an orderly fashion. If your subject has no reason to evade you and doesn't realize you are searching for him or her, that person is probably going to be easy to find. You may not be in a hurry and can afford to write letters and wait for replies. On the other hand, if you are in a hurry and do not care about cost, you might want to consider using an information broker, in which case you must have a correct name, Social Security number, or last known address in order for the computer to find information about your subject. The more information you have, the easier it is to locate the person by computer.

In case you do not have a name, date of birth, Social Security number, or last known address, you may want to register your search in a computer registry. I operate such a nationwide missing persons registry that is capable of matching two or more persons who are searching for each other—anywhere in the world! You can register at www.reunion.com or write Reunion Network, P.O. Box 290333, Nashville, TN 37229-0333. (For more information, write Nationwide Locating Services, U.F.O., Inc, P.O. Box 290333, Nashville, TN 37229-0333.)

Before you decide which method suits your particular search, study all the methods available and determine what will help you most. Follow these eight guidelines to get started:

1. Identify the problem on paper, preferably using checklists, with all known persons who may be involved, what you know about each person, what you need to find out about each person, and so forth (see sample checklists in Chapter Fifteen).

2. Evaluate the information assembled on the checklists and decide who may have additional information about the person you are searching for.

3. Review and analyze information obtained from the Internet. Register with registries (www.reunion.com), and utilize newsgroups and chatrooms by asking questions.

4. Plan where you need to go to obtain additional information you need: library, courthouse, federal building, neighborhood. Identify where the data may be located.

5. Get into the habit of writing down everything. A daily log of each new clue will make searching easier. Always include date and time, who you spoke with, what was said, and what information you learned.

6. Practice asking questions. Become aware of how you ask questions that get you results—useful information. With practice, you will be able to conduct an interview with a total stranger, making the interviewee feel comfortable and relaxed. The secret to asking questions that produce results is a combination of good attitude, controlled tone of voice, nonthreatening mannerisms, and awareness of your appearance.

7. Learn to be a good listener. To get someone to tell you what you need to know, you may have to listen to unre-

lated matters. Be patient and wait for an opportunity to present itself. The ability to recognize opportunity and to act on the opportunity immediately is a skill that can be developed with practice. Actually, it's best to lead someone in another direction, away from the issue at hand, before asking what you really need to know. You may have to talk about most anything, but if you play your cards right, the opportunity will present itself, you will take advantage of the opportunity, and the person you are talking to will never notice that you asked.

8. Evaluate and analyze each piece of information to be sure that you have not overlooked any clues, and eliminate any information that is not vital to your search. This will allow you to profile your missing person. What do you actually know? What additional information do you need to find this person?

The most important thing to remember as you read this book is not only the techniques, but the underlying principle— that an almost infinite number of angles can be explored to get the information you need. Be creative with your own variations of these techniques as you go along. Mold them to fit your specific needs.

Some typical sources of information to get you started include the following (in no particular order):

Internet: white pages, yellow pages, e-mail directories, Websites, registries, and newsgroups.

Records: marriage, divorce, birth and death, driving, criminal, change of address, insurance, voter registration, real estate, military, alumni, fraternity and sorority, school, cemetery, funeral home, adoption, hospital, census, legal, and immigration.

Documents: business licenses, birth and death certificates, legal notices, and obituaries.

Organizations: unions, trade, professional, and civic organizations, and religious institutions.

People: friends, family, neighbors, community members, teachers, and co-workers. (When contacting people, look for both current and former relationships.)

Finding missing persons is nothing more than a combination of knowledge, experience, and resources. Once you understand and master the fundamentals of basic investigative techniques, you should be able to find almost anyone.

The foundation of investigation is the ability to analyze your information. Until you are experienced at this, begin by making a list of what information you have to work with and what you can do with it. Now take what you have written and examine it closely. All information can be examined and evaluated. Analyzing is nothing more than taking a closer look. No matter how little you have to start with, there is always something you can do. In order to know where to look for additional information, it is necessary to have a thorough understanding of public records. Whether you are searching for a criminal, an heir or beneficiary, a witness, someone who owes money, someone for civil process, a relative, or a friend, there is always a way.

I assume you are adventurous and like to explore. Think of your search as a new adventure. Pretend this is a treasure hunt and the treasure is the missing person. Consider each obstacle as a new opportunity, and don't get discouraged. If you are not determined to find your missing person, you will probably give up easily. Do not let this happen! Keep a positive attitude and whenever a plan fails, re-examine the plan and try it again, but do something different. This is persistence. As far as I'm concerned, "no" only means "maybe." I don't give up easily and I don't get discouraged. When things don't go like I plan them, I just "back up ten and try again."

Allow for unexpected obstacles, and be prepared to deal with them. Remember that there is usually another way to accomplish your goal. Don't get discouraged if at first you do not succeed—just keep trying.

5

Gathering Information

To EFFECTIVELY gather useful information, a workable plan of action is necessary, regardless of what type of information you need: personal profile, business profile, or a court case. The same applies to finding missing persons. The eight guidelines elaborated on in Chapter Four are worth summarizing here:

1. Write down all the information you know about the person you seek (see sample checklists in Chapter Fifteen).
2. Evaluate the information you have and decide who might have additional information.
3. Review and analyze information obtained from the Internet.
4. Plan where you need to go to get your missing information.
5. Keep a daily log of everything related to your search.
6. Practice asking effective questions.
7. Learn to be a good listener.
8. Evaluate and analyze each piece of information that is not vital to your search and profile your missing person. What do you actually know? What additional information do you need in order to find this person?

With everything you learn, whether it be from talking to other people, reading newspapers, or looking through records and documents, remember that the purpose of the search is to obtain facts. Never lose sight of your goal. Many of the facts you gather will seem to be irrelevant, but you can never be sure which seemingly irrelevant facts will turn out to be important. Regardless of what you do, the only thing that really counts is the facts you gather.

Data Collection

A fisherman may not catch a fish, but he will continue to try different locations, different bait, and different techniques until he finally catches a fish. You must apply the same strategy of persistence and determination. Select a target such as a sec-retary or receptionist and make a simple phone call. Give this person the opportunity to tell you all about the company, the boss, and whatever else you may need to know, without directly asking for this information. You can easily say, "Oh, by the way, I was just wondering if. . . ."

For example, recently I needed some information from an office that was not allowed to release it. The receptionist told me she could not let me have the list of names I needed and that it was not for the public. It was 3:30 on a Friday afternoon. My time was running out, and I needed that information within the hour.

After refusing to fax me the list of names I needed, I asked the receptionist, "By the way, what building are you in?" She told me. I talked about something completely unrelated to what I actually wanted, just as a diversion, saying something like "that office is in a great location." I thanked her for her help and never let on that her refusal had bothered me.

My first plan had been unsuccessful. Now it was time for another approach. Banking on the sage advice that you should treat people better than they treat you, I didn't burn the bridge

I had just crossed. Who knows? I may have to turn around and cross it again.

At a time like this it really pays to have friends and contacts. The more sources of information, the easier the search. I just happened to have a friend who worked in that same building and owed me a favor. "Would it be too much trouble for you to go to an office in your building and pick up a list of names I need today?" I asked. "Sure," she responded.

My friend went to the office and talked to the receptionist who had told me on the phone that she could not let me see or have a copy of the list I needed. My friend asked how much the list would cost, paid the receptionist $10, and faxed it to me—no questions asked. I made my deadline, without leaving my desk. How many people would have tried to get that list after the receptionist said she could not let anyone have it? How many people would have tried another plan? How many people would have walked away empty-handed? Do you see my point? I don't give up or get discouraged. I realize that obstacles are merely opportunities in disguise. And you must do the same.

Locating Your Missing Person

To find the person you are searching for, it may be necessary to locate a friend or relative of the missing person to get information as to his or her whereabouts. That kind of information about friends, relatives, or associates may be found in such unlikely places as a newsletter, a church directory, a trade journal, school yearbooks, club or organization membership directories, professional associations or licensing boards, or even a newspaper clipping of a funeral. Perhaps a pall bearer at a funeral is the best friend of your target. A former employer or co-worker may provide information. I have even found people and information simply by calling the court clerk's office and asking if my target person ever filed for divorce. This information may not be available with a phone call in every state or jurisdiction, but there is usually a way to obtain information of some type.

As an example, let's name your target Harry Mott. Here's what we know about him: his name is Harry Mott, and his last known city of residence was Nashville, Tennessee. Let's say that is all the information you have to begin your search. From this information alone, here is what you can do:

Analyze and evaluate the data; Recognize that the name Mott is not common. While checking the Nashville phone directory to see how many Motts are listed, you find out that there are only a few and none are named Harry. This tells you several things: he may have moved away; he may have an unlisted phone number; he may be deceased; or he may be related to some of the Motts who are listed.

Eliminate data that are not relevant. What should we do first? It seems that we have two choices: search for a death certificate, or call some of the Motts listed in the phone book. Either of these methods is acceptable.

You can obtain a death record by looking up the Social Security Death Index (www.ancestry.com/ssdi) on the World Wide Web. There are 92 million death records available through my computer simply by entering a name. In fact, I can find all persons who have died between 1940 and 1993 with that name. Once I find a record, I will have the person's date of birth, Social Security number, place of birth, and last known address.

You can write or visit the Mormon church library of genealogical records. These records, going back before 1968, can be accessed over the Internet (www.lds.org) and downloaded for free.

You can write your state Department of Vital Statistics (cost: about $10) or go to their Website (when applicable).

Records

Our government feels that record keeping is a necessity; therefore records exist, both public and private, on just about any subject you might be looking for. Have you ever considered how many records exist on you? Almost all of your activities are recorded somewhere.

Although most of the following records (listed in random order) exist on the average American citizen, not all are available for inspection by anyone except the next of kin. Go to the Privacy Act Website (www.livelinks.com) to find out about the laws restricting records.

1. Birth certificate (P in most states)
2. Birth medical records (N)
3. Baptism/church/religious records (P)
4. Pre-school/kindergarten records (N)
5. Activities (swimming lessons; music lessons; art lessons; Girl and Boy Scouts, etc.) (N)
6. Medical records (N)
7. Social Security number (N)
8. Bank account (savings) (N)
9. Health insurance (N)
10. School records (N)
11. Driver's license/traffic tickets/accidents (P)
12. Employment (N)
13. College (N)
14. Checking account (N)
15. Alumni association (N)
16. Fraternal/sorority organizations (N)
17. Loan/debts/credit cards/credit (N)
18. Vehicle/vehicle insurance (P/N)
19. Voter registration (P, most states)
20. Military service records/enlistment/discharge (N)
21. Marriage(s) (P)
22. Divorce(s)/child custody/child support/alimony (P)

23. Utility/electricity/water/gas/phone (N)
24. Hobbies/clubs/organizations (P)
25. Professional licensing (P)
26. Business license (P)
27. Taxes (real estate) (P)
28. Bankruptcy (P)
29. Lawsuit/judgment/lien (P)
30. Mortgage (P)
31. Property/real/tangible/other (P)
32. Investments/stocks/dividends/other (N)
33. Insurance/homeowners/life/accident/vehicle/other (N)
34. Disability claims (N)
35. Workers' compensation claims (P)
36. Unemployment records (N)
37. Employment tax records (N)
38. Income tax records (N)
39. Retirement/CDs/annuities (N)
40. Corporate records (P)
41. Death certificate (P)
42. Funeral/burial (P)
43. Will (P)

(P = public record, N = nonpublic record but the next of kin may have access)

I hope your brain is clicking with ideas of what public records you can look for. As you can see, the paper trail seems to be unending, even after death. Use your imagination and see how many records you can find, both public and nonpublic, on your missing person. Here are a few to consider:

Credit Information (www.reunion.com to link to NIC)

The Fair Credit Reporting Act provides that credit information may be requested from a consumer reporting agency only for certain permissible purposes, including:

- In response to the order of a court having jurisdiction to issue such an order;
- In accordance with the written instructions of the consumer to whom it relates (a signed release);
- To use the information in connection with a credit transaction involving the consumer on whom the information is furnished;
- To use the information in connection with the extension of credit to the consumer;
- To use the information in connection with the review or collection of an account of the consumer;
- To use the information for employment purposes;
- To use the information in connection with the underwriting of insurance involving the consumer; or
- To use the information in connection with a determination of governmental instrumentality required by law to consider an applicant's financial responsibility or status.

Credit information may be purchased by the consumer involved or any person who meets the above criteria. It is best to have permission in writing from the person for whom you are requesting the information. In case of a dispute over the legality of your request, you will be able to prove that you had permission to run the report. Otherwise, you might find yourself liable for a lawsuit involving invasion of privacy, among other things. Credit information is not something to be taken lightly. Federal laws are very serious, and persons found guilty of obtaining credit information without a legitimate, permissible purpose may be fined and imprisoned.

If you need information on someone and do not have a permissible reason for obtaining the full credit report, you may consider obtaining only the "header" or "footer" information from the report (available through information broker/computer databases), which does not include accounts, only vital information such as name, address, age, Social Security number, employer, spouse, and names of other persons who have inquired about the report previously. This information can be invaluable. I once found a man as a result of contacting a car dealer who was listed on the footer information of the credit report because he had inquired about the man. By contacting the car dealer and talking to the salesman who had sold the man a car, I was able to locate his current employer and new address. At his office I asked to speak to him, was told he was "in the field," and was given his beeper number.

Almost everyone you give personal information to sells it to someone else for a profit, especially credit bureaus. Credit bureaus know not only your accounts but also all inquiries made about you by other people. They sell your Social Security number, your date of birth, your spouse's name, every address you have used with credit information, and even your employment information. They even allow their information to be available through databases.

Medical Records

The Medical Information Bureau collects physician and hospital records on more than 12 million Americans and Canadians and is the largest computerized repository of available medical records. The files also contain information on drug and alcohol dependency, psychological tests, and HIV test results.

Medical records may be stored in another state and recorded on microfilm. It is not unusual for medical records to be destroyed after the death of a physician or the closing of a medical facility. Some states destroy records after seven or more years due to lack of storage space.

Each state may have a law regarding requesting medical information, but it has been my experience that all I need is a "medical authorization" for release of medical records, signed either by the person whose records are being requested or that person's next of kin.

You may also want to look for a workers' compensation claim. Anyone who may have been involved in a work-related injury probably filed a report of some type and you should not have any trouble obtaining a copy. Check a telephone book for the state office that handles these claims.

Landlord Evictions

There is a database called Evictalert that contains records of persons reported by their landlords for failure to pay rent or for damage to rental property. Available through National Credit Information (NCI, which is accessible by certain professional legitimate businesses only), it has not been around a long time and is not complete, but it is a database worth checking if you are looking for someone who owes money or has a criminal past.

Financial Records

FINCEN is the federal government's Financial Central Record Database, which contains recorded financial transactions of every American citizen. FINCEN is fed information from your bank account, credit card, taxes, and any other transaction that appears on paper. Accessible only to authorized personnel, it is said to be the "granddaddy of all databases."

Where Do You Find Information?

From courthouses to churches, directories to death certificates, there is a wealth of information just waiting to be tapped. Here are a few of the more common—and helpful—places to begin.

Courthouses

If you are searching for records related to property, try the tax assessor's office for property tax records, or the registrar of deeds office for deeds to property including the history of ownership. (While you're at it, why not search for other persons with the same last name and see if any of them are related to the person you seek?)

If the family you seek still owns the house, the registrar of deeds will show no record of a transaction transferring ownership of the property. If your missing person has sold the property outright, or is holding a second mortgage, the county recorder will almost always have a record of it. In the latter case, the county recorder and the present owner should both have the seller's new address. If the property was sold outright, look for the real estate office that handled the transaction, the mortgage company that arranged the loan, a bank, a notary, or an attorney. Contact the new owner and/or neighbors and ask for the name of friends or relatives who might know what happened to the person you seek.

Department of Motor Vehicles

Every state has a Department of Motor Vehicles (DMV), which maintains current and historical records of all drivers and their automobiles. Most states' records are accessible through a database. A quick look at your own driver's license shows how useful these records can be. Your full name, current address, date of birth, possibly a Social Security number (in some states this is the driver's license number), and your physical description are all right there. A check of your driving history will reveal accidents, tickets (even in other states), and dates of any violations or arrests. Although these records may not be considered public information in every state, most DMVs will release this data if there is "good cause." Most states require as little information as the person's name and date of birth. Databases also allow vehicle license plates and/or vehicle identification numbers to be traced. Information brokers may have access to records using a name only.

Libraries (sunsite.berkeley.edu/Libweb/usa-state.html)

Finding information in a library is like finding a buried treasure. It's there, but it's up to you to uncover it. The reference librarian can direct you to the source that will be the most helpful. Of course, the main branch will have more information than a smaller branch.

Always be prepared for unanticipated expenses, making sure to have plenty of change for parking and photocopies, a pen and tablet to take notes with, and a checklist of what to look for.

Before visiting the library, call to see if it has current, as well as older, editions of city/suburban directories and cross-reference directories or other materials you anticipate needing. Ask what information is available on CD-ROM, microfilm, and microfiche. Are the photocopy machines working? How much do they charge for making photocopies? What are the library hours? Are researchers available, and if so are they volunteers or do they charge a fee? How much? It may be cost effective to pay someone to do your work for you. If the public library doesn't have what you need, consider a university library.

The reference section of a public library, especially the main library, contains valuable reference material in book form, on computer, on microfiche, and on microfilm. Older records and documents may be found at the state archives. Local courthouses also maintain some form of storage for old records and may also have archives. Seldom are records completely destroyed.

The reference librarian is extremely knowledgeable and will assist you if you ask for help. Most libraries have access to the Internet. Reference librarians are usually available to help you get on-line, and although they may not be experts, they can help you get started browsing the Web. If you are unable to visit a library in person or by Internet, you may request information by mail. Some libraries have volunteers who can research for you. Call and ask for the price of photocopies and the name of the person you should contact.

Telephone books, cross-reference (crisscross) directories, yearbooks, and city/suburban directories may go back thirty or more years. If you have an old address of a missing person, check the year before and after the person resided there. Are the same neighbors still there? Are they listed in a current directory? Finding a former neighbor could be the key to finding your missing person.

Computers may be available to access an index to old or new newspaper articles, such as birth and death notices, marriages, and divorces. Check with your library about what databases or other computer services might be available. Mormon church libraries are great for genealogical research.

One of the leading database vendors is Dialog Information Services, Inc. DIALOG offers more than 400 academic, business, and newspaper/periodical databases containing more than 200 million records. Another large vendor is Mead Data Central, which offers LEXIS, a vast database system for lawyers, and NEXIS, a system of newspaper, periodical, and business-oriented databases. On-line searches can be costly, however. Some will offer lower rates during specific time periods, but you will need to check out the details before choosing this route.

Trade and professional associations and other nonprofit organizations are almost always willing to help you. To find the most relevant group for your search, look in the subject and location guides of the Encyclopedia of Associations and the National Trade and Professional Associations of the United States. Then contact the research director or newsletter editor of the group. The Directory of Experts, Authorities & Spokespersons is the annual volume used by radio and TV talk-show hosts to find people to appear on their shows. It contains a number of offbeat specialties not found in other directories.

Maps, telephone books, city/suburban directories, historical publications, professional directories, who's who directories, newspaper articles, and census records are but a few of the sources of information that should be available at a public library.

For example, assume that you have the last name of the person you're looking for. While researching old city directories, you notice that a particular individual disappeared after a certain year. This could mean he did not have a telephone, perhaps he died, or maybe he moved away.

If you have an address, try making a few calls to the neighbors (using city and cross-reference directories). After locating a neighbor who remembered the family, you may find that your missing person has moved. Now what?

Five things are possible: the house was sold outright; the house was sold but the owner holds the mortgage; the owner may be renting out the house; the missing person was a renter himself; or a relative may occupy the house.

In any case, what you have uncovered thus far will lead you to the courthouse, another helpful source discussed earlier in this chapter.

Mailing Lists

Private companies offer mailing lists of Americans divided into almost any category imaginable—age groups, professions, businesses, households, consumers, geographic regions. They can be categorized as to people who buy insurance, people who hunt or fish, people who own cars, or people who order from catalogs. Mailing lists are available to anyone who wants to pay for them. You may order lists on disks or printed labels.

To request information about mailing lists, look in your yellow pages under direct marketing or mail services. Or see if your main public library has phone and address directories available on CD-ROM.

State Archives and Libraries

Every state maintains archival information for that state, which includes old newspapers, telephone books, current (and past) city directories from every major city in the state, and state and county courthouse documents. Records are available of all persons from that state who actively served in the military during each war. Most of the records will be at least twenty years old. This is not the place to go for current information. But if you need to trace back many years, this is definitely where you should look. Records are indexed, microfilmed, microfiched, and kept in original condition. State archives and libraries are excellent for genealogical and adoption information. Some states have birth indexes, which list everyone born in those states.

The Library of Congress (www.loc.gov)

The Library of Congress, located in Washington, DC, is the largest library in the United States. The Library of Congress can be accessed over the Internet (www.loc.gov), or the National Reference Service will help you over the phone: (202) 707-5522. If you need research from the Library of Congress, there are private researchers who will help you, for a fee.

National Archives (www.nara.gov)

The National Archives is a federal repository whose records date back to the 1700s. It is available on the Internet (www.nara.gov) and provides a wealth of information, including military, census, older FBI investigations, and family background records. In addition to the national headquarters in Washington, DC, there are twelve regional branches located across the United States.

There is a request for information form that may be completed and sent to one of these libraries. For $10, they will research a name for you.

Contact information for the National Archives and its regional branches can be found in Chapter Fifteen.

Telephone Books

The logical place to begin looking for someone is in a telephone book; but of course you will not find someone with an unlisted number, who has remarried and has a name you do not know, or who has moved to another city. Nevertheless, the telephone book can provide names of family members who live in the same city.

The Internet is ideal for looking up telephone numbers or e-mail addresses. There are Websites for yellow pages (www.ypo.com), white pages (www.whowhere.com), toll free numbers (inter800.com), and e-mail addresses (www.four11. com). These databases can search by city or nationwide, but are only helpful if the business or individual is listed.

Old telephone books are valuable because the person you are looking for may have been listed previously. Therefore you may find a former address, which will lead you to the neighbors. Possibly a neighbor who remembers your missing person can provide you with information as to the individual's whereabouts.

If you are an adoptee searching for your birth parents, use a directory for the year before, the year of, and the year after your birth. One of the listings may be your grandparents. Perhaps your parents were still living at home at the time of your birth and did not have a phone listed in their name. If you know the city where your birth parents once lived, check directories for the surrounding cities within a one-hundred-mile radius.

Looking up a last name is easy. If you find more than a few that match, you might want to write one letter, photocopy it, and mail it to all of the people with the right last name. This would keep you from making numerous phone calls.

However, if you have only a partial name or a nickname, you may not recognize the name that is listed because it is not the one you are looking for. Over the years I have learned to look for any name that contains the initial of the name I had.

For example, say I needed to locate Edward Tillman. The phone book does not list an Edward Tillman; however, there is a C. E. Tillman. Edward might be his middle name.

Ask directory assistance to check for a listing in the entire area code you want checked, not just the city. You may at least determine if the person has an unlisted number.

Computer Database Information Services

It is not necessary to own a computer or even to be computer literate to obtain information by computer. Information broker services are available to sell you information from their computer databases. However, more and more information is becoming available on the Internet. If you don't have a computer, most libraries offer free Internet access. This doesn't mean you will definitely find what you need on the Internet, and when you reach a dead end, there are thousands of information brokers and search services. Most of these services provide the same information at competitive prices, ranging from five to fifty dollars.

In this Information Age, a surname search is possible throughout the United States with a computer database. Nationwide Locating Services provides millions of phone records, addresses, name searches, death record searches (1940–1994), and a world of other information that may be requested by phone, fax, or in writing. Payment in advance is accepted with a credit card, check, or money order.

Most professional brokers who provide information to attorneys, private investigators, collection agencies, credit services, property managers, and for pre-employment screening use a gateway service called National Credit Information (NCI). Through this one service, access to the following information is available: Consumer credit information from more than 1,000 credit bureaus containing more than 350 million files; Social Security number tracing and verification, for name and address identification, more than 300 million files; Address identification and updates, including information on Social Security numbers, employer information, present and previous addresses, more than 250 million files; Nationwide crisscross for cross-referencing names, phone numbers, and addresses, including searches for identifying neighbors' addresses and phone numbers, more than 92 million files; Nationwide driving record information, providing validity of license, moving violations, arrests, and reported addresses assigned to the license number you provide; Nationwide driver's license number search, provided from only the subject's name, date of birth, and the state you wished searched; Nationwide alpha name search, provided from the subject's name, last known address or state you want searched, to determine the driver's license number, record, and vehicle ownership; Nationwide license plate identification search, provided from any plate/tag number you request and the state to be searched, to determine the ownership of the vehicle and all addresses assigned to that plate number and its vehicle identification number; Commercial business profiles describing a business's credit history, profit and loss history, length of operation, type of business, officers, banking and loan references, payment trends, number of employees, sales volume, and more; Nationwide workers' compensation claim searches on your subject by state, to determine number and type of any claims filed; Nationwide business crisscross cross-referencing business phone number, name, and address information, containing more than eight million files; Nationwide criminal history record searches, providing any criminal convictions from the county you wish searched on the subject, or state you wish searched, or any federal criminal convictions at the county or state level (not all criminal records are available by computer at this time); Federal Aviation Administration searches by tail number or pilot name for owner registration information; and Death record searches through the Social Security Administration's Master Death Record File, more than 41 million records.

Not everyone will qualify to use NCI, which constantly adds new databases to its offerings. You must be a legitimate business with a legal reason for needing the information. If you qualify, you will be allowed access immediately. You can access NCI through www.reunion.com.

Public Records

Each court and each jurisdiction should have basically the same types of records available; however; each state, county, parish, township, city, or court may call the public offices by different names. Types of public records available at local courthouses and city halls include:

- Registrar of Deeds: Property deeds recorded; Liens/judgments against property/owner;
- Property Tax Assessor: Appraisals; Maps; Properties owned by individuals or businesses listed by name and location; History of ownership of property;
- County Court Clerk: Vehicle license information; Marriage records; Business licenses; Business taxes;
- Voter Registration: Election records; Registered voters;
- Circuit Court Clerk (or equivalent): Divorce; Adoption; Name changes; Child support enforcement; Lawsuits (involving claims over or under $10,000);
- Chancery Court Clerk (or equivalent): Litigation; Judgments; Lawsuits; Divorce; Adoption;
- Probate Court Clerk (or equivalent): Wills; Estates; Committals; Property deeds; Name changes;
- Trustee: Collection of property taxes;
- Criminal Court Clerk: Criminal arrests; Warrants; Court dates; Court costs;
- County Health Department: Records relating to health; Vital records; Birth certificates; and
- Traffic Violation Bureau: Traffic tickets.

Check the telephone book for public offices available in your city or the city of your search. Don't hesitate to call a public office and ask what records are available and if there is a charge for obtaining copies of their files. Ask if any of the information is available on-line. If you want to write a letter requesting the information by mail, you will need the correct mailing address and contact person, as well as information regarding any costs (some of this information is provided in Chapter Fifteen). It is not always necessary to obtain information in person.

State records that might be available to the public include (not all records in every department are public in every state): driver's license history and vehicle registration and title; corporations' annual reports and charters; UCC filings: secured collateral for loans; birth certificates; death records; birth index; marriage licenses; unclaimed property; education department; election commission; parole board; employment security; health department; human services department; mental health department; military department; public service department; revenue department; personnel department; state bureau of investigation; department of transportation; veterans' affairs department; and professional licensing boards.

Federal records you might be able to access include: U.S. Bankruptcy Court; Department of Defense, military branches/locating services; Federal Bureau of Investigation (some investigations are available through the Freedom of Information Act; others can be found at National Archives); Housing and Urban Development; Internal Revenue Service (the Office of Disclosure may forward a letter to a relative); Department of Labor; Transportation Department; Treasury Department; U.S. Postal Service; Social Security (may forward a letter to next of kin); Veterans' Affairs Department (veterans' claims for benefits); and Department of Agriculture.

A list of federal agencies that might help you in your search can be found in the Reference Section.

Post Office Records (www.usps.gov)

The U.S. Postal Service will no longer allow you to request copies of change of address cards filed by other people. Instead, you should mail a letter to the last address you have for the person, being sure to write "Address Correction Requested" on the envelope. It should be returned to you with the current information.

Voter Registration Records

The person you're looking for may be a regular voter. If so, a voter registration card can be a simple way to locate vital information. These records may be located at the county courthouse and should contain the following information: full name, address, date of birth, place of birth, employer, and voting district.

6

From My Files: Real Searches for Real People

SEARCHES FOR missing loved ones are endless. Many searches result from curiosity about one's heritage; some for necessity; some for medical reasons; and some for identity.

Regardless of the reason for the search, the need to fill a void, the need to feel complete, the need for information is vital to human development. To suppress the desire to find a missing loved one only causes problems that may surface in other forms.

Let me encourage you to find your missing loved one and live with the truth instead of the unknown. Whatever you find is better than not knowing. Be prepared to accept whatever you find, because your life will change forever. You can let go of any feelings of anger or frustration that often accompany the unknown, allowing you to feel complete at last.

Sample Cases

A Mother Searches for Her Kidnapped Daughter

> *Dear Norma,*
>
> My daughter Bonnie was only six when I last saw her fifteen years ago. I had custody of my daughter

after a bitter divorce. My ex-husband had visitation rights and I was ordered by the court to allow him visits. Fifteen years ago he took Bonnie for a visit and disappeared with her. At first he would let her call me, but would cut her off before she could tell me where they were. After a few months, she was not allowed to contact me again.

I reported Bonnie's disappearance to the local sheriff's office. I called my ex-husband's relatives. I contacted schools and did everything I could think of. Nothing helped. The sheriff's office entered my daughter into a national computer for missing children. The local law enforcement agency contacted the F.B.I. Warrants were issued for the arrest of my ex-husband. I called them regularly, but they never had any news. Eventually I gave up. I never expected to see Bonnie again. I did not believe anyone was trying to find her. No one cared.

I remarried and had other children. One night, my ex-husband returned and set my house on fire with all of us inside. Fortunately, we were unharmed. This man was very vindictive. I feared for the safety of my daughter.

Even though I have exhausted all known means of locating my daughter, when I saw you on television, my hope was renewed. I thought I had done all that I could do, but something made me write you. Can you please help me?

—SANDY

≈ ≈ ≈

Dear Sandy,

Unfortunately your situation is very common. Thousands of children have disappeared as a result of noncustodial parental kidnapping. In order to disappear completely, the kidnapper must totally break all ties with existing family members, friends, associates, and employers and begin a new identity. This is very difficult. To begin a new life with no ties to the old life requires a lot of planning and preparation. It helps to have a lot of money available, because no paper trails to bank accounts can be left behind. How can someone disappear and not leave a paper trail? No more insurance, no checking or savings accounts, no mortgage, no credit, no driver's license, no vehicle registration, no voter's registration, and no contact with anyone.

Choosing to disappear and change identities is a tedious task. A new birth certificate, Social Security number, and resume are issued. You are purged of your name, your history, your friends and your family. You will live among strangers in a place quite your own.
—NORMA

> ### Analyze the problem and look for the seed for your solution.

Bonnie's father is running from law enforcement. He was a known criminal, guilty not only of kidnapping, but also of arson. More than likely he had several aliases and had changed Bonnie's identity by assuming the name of someone who died who was approximately Bonnie's age. (A common way to change one's identity.) Regardless of who he claimed to be and who he claimed Bonnie to be, he made a mistake. When Sandy wrote me, I sent her one of my missing person questionnaires to complete. I was surprised to see that she entered Bonnie's Social Security number. The father had inadvertently neglected to apply for a new Social Security number for Bonnie. At twenty-one, Bonnie was still using the same Social Security number that was issued to her under her real name. This was the seed for the solution.

Bonnie was unaware that she was a kidnapping victim. Her father told her that her mother did not love her or want her any more and that was why she was living with him. Even though her heart was broken, at age six, Bonnie believed her father. She remembered wondering if her mother ever thought about her.

She grew up a victim of kidnapping and child abuse. Her father did not love her and did not really want her; he took Bonnie only to hurt her mother. He was very abusive, physically and mentally. He left Bonnie with strangers and disappeared. A criminal who was running from the law, he was arrested for other offenses; the kidnapping warrant never surfaced.

At the time I located Bonnie, she was living with her boyfriend in Dallas, Texas, and attending college. She was fearful of her father finding her, even though the boyfriend's family was very protective of her. Bonnie thought I was playing a cruel joke on her and that her father had actually hired me to locate her.

When I convinced Bonnie that I was looking for her on behalf of her mother, she was ecstatic. For the first time in fifteen years she was told that her mother loved her and wanted to find her.

A television show had contacted me to arrange a reunion for the Thanksgiving holidays. They requested an emotional situation with a happy ending. This was the perfect choice. Bonnie agreed to surprise her mother on live television.

Getting Sandy to go on television to talk about her daughter's disappearance was not easy. She could not talk about Bonnie without crying and thus was embarrassed. I suggested that she might give hope to other mothers in similar situations and possibly could appeal to Bonnie, if she were watching, or to someone who might know of her whereabouts. Reluctantly, Sandy agreed to discuss her daughter's kidnapping on television.

During an emotional interview, Sandy was asked on camera what she would say to Bonnie if Bonnie were watching. She buried her face in her hands and cried, "Just let me know you are alive."

The host then exclaimed, "Today is your day; here is your baby!"
Bonnie then rushed out from the wings to meet her mother. Needless
to say, there was not a dry eye in the studio. Chances are, there
weren't many in the viewers' homes, either.

Bonnie and Sandy had a lot of catching up to do. Thirty mem-
bers of the family gathered for Thanksgiving dinner, bringing gifts to
Bonnie to welcome her home. She met brothers and sisters she did
not know she had.

After the reunion, Bonnie returned to Dallas and married her
boyfriend. I attended the wedding. A year later, Bonnie gave birth to
a daughter.

A Sister Looks for Her Brother

Dear Norma,

Seventeen years ago my brother and his wife separated. They had two small children. While my
brother was home for a visit, he was notified that his
year-old-baby had drowned in the bathtub. The last
time I saw my brother was when I took him to the airport to return for his daughter's funeral. He was never
heard from again. He was deeply depressed over his
failed marriage, and the death of the baby was devastating. I do not know whether my brother is dead or
alive. I do not know why he never contacted our family again. I have tried to locate him, but no one has
seen or heard from him since the baby's funeral. I do
not know where to turn. I want to find my brother.
His family loves him and misses him very much. I am
enclosing his full name, date of birth, Social Security
number, and last known address.
—DIANE

∽ ∽ ∽

Dear Diane,

Seventeen years is a long time for someone not to contact his family. I suspect that there must have been a family problem you failed to mention. Ordinarily, people do not leave a happy, well-adjusted home. I understand your brother's depression, and possible guilt, surrounding his child's death. As hard as it is, you must consider that your brother might have suffered a nervous breakdown or has amnesia. He might even be dead. If those extreme possibilities are not proven, he may be on file in a computer database.

The average person will leave a paper trail. Your brother probably has a vehicle and a driver's license. He may be located with only his Social Security number. If he is not deliberately hiding, your brother can probably be located easily.

—NORMA

Because this woman provided me with her brother's full name, date of birth, last known address, and Social Security number, I was able to search a computer database. A simple search of on-line phone directories or e-mail directories may be all that is necessary to find your missing person.

An Abandoned Son Searches for His Mother

Dear Norma,

The youngest of six children, I am a thirty-year-old married man who has not seen or heard from my mother since I was ten. My father was very abusive and an alcoholic. My mother married him when she was sixteen. I love my mother very much and I miss her every day.

I worry whether she is alive. I wonder what happened to her. She did not tell us anything and has not contacted us since her disappearance. She worked as a waitress and did not return home after work one night. Living with the unknown has almost driven me crazy. I have had three nervous breakdowns as a result.

My father's mother raised us. My father, who is now deceased, abused us. My grandmother loved us and was good to us, but she could not take the place of our mother.

Even though everything has been done that can be done as far as reporting my mother as a missing person to the police, in twenty years no one has found out anything. There has not been a trail to follow. I want to believe she is alive. I must know what happened to her. Please help me!

Enclosed is a copy of her birth certificate, a copy of her Social Security card, a photograph, and her father's death notice (he died last year and I assume she does not know).

—JERRY

≈ ≈ ≈

Dear Jerry,

Of all the missing persons I have received letters about, yours is one of the saddest. I know it has been traumatic living with the unknown. Your imagination has probably run from one extreme to another.

I can understand your mother wanting to get away from an abusive, alcoholic husband, but I cannot imagine her leaving six children to be abused by him. This makes me wonder whether your mother left voluntarily or involuntarily.

If she left voluntarily, she must have thought only of herself, not her children. Based on the information you furnished, it is possible that your father could have murdered her and her body has never been found. I'm sure that thought has also occurred to you.

I'm sure that if your mother is located, you will be healed of all the hurt, frustration, and anger that has resulted from not knowing what happened.

—NORMA

Jerry furnished me his mother's full name, date of birth, last known address, and Social Security number. If she left voluntarily, she probably changed her name. If she left involuntarily, there is probably no paper trail. If there is no trail whatsoever after twenty years, Jerry's mother may be deceased.

If she left voluntarily and changed her identity, did she change her Social Security number? Probably not. The seed for the solution to this problem is the Social Security number. By running this number through my computer database, Jerry's mother was located immediately. Instead of Joan, she is now Jane Brown, married and living in Georgia. (Jerry's mother never divorced her first husband.)

I attempted to contact Jane Brown by phone. I left my name and phone number several times on an answering machine, but no call was returned. Eventually I drove to Georgia and located the house. I spoke to neighbors and showed them the photograph. The neighbors identified the photograph as the woman who lived at that address. I knocked on the door and a man (who turned out to be Jane's husband) stated that Jane was not home from work yet. He did not seem curious about who I was or what I wanted, as are most of the people I encounter. I showed him the photograph. He said he had never seen that woman before.

Did I have the wrong person? If so, why did she have the same Social Security number? He did not invite me in. I asked if he minded if I waited for her and he said no, so I waited in my car. When Jane arrived, I told her who I was and that her son wanted to find his mother. She denied that she was the right person, even though she had the two moles on her face that Jerry had described and looked like the woman in the photograph (she denied being that woman). She said she did not have any children. This woman was convinced she was the wrong person, but I believed she was the right person. She even showed me her driver's license with the same date of birth as Jerry's mother's birth certificate. I showed her this and she still denied being that person. She showed me her Social Security number and I showed her the one Jerry sent me. She wondered why that "other woman" was using her number. Jerry's mother was in denial. I had never run into a case like this before. Apparently, the woman had begun a new life, pretending the old life never existed. She was in a state of total denial.

Jane never admitted anything. In fact, she was convinced that I had the wrong person and told me not to contact her again. I showed her Jerry's letter, but it did not faze her. I asked if I could take her picture to show Jerry, and she agreed. Of course, this was my proof that she was in fact the right person.

I did not have the heart to call Jerry and tell him that I found his mother, who did not want any contact with him. I decided to call her sister Liz instead. When I contacted the sister and explained the situation, she thought I must have made a mistake. I told her to be quiet while I made a conference call. I called Jane and talked to her while her sister listened. Jane asked me why I was calling, as she had already told me I had the wrong person. I wanted her sister to hear this for herself. Jane said there was no need for me to contact her again, that she was definitely not the right person. I told Jane I just wanted to be sure that she had not changed her mind and offer her my phone number. "I won't need your number," she said.

Liz was convinced that this voice was indeed her sister. She was stunned. After a few weeks, Liz got up the nerve to tell Jerry, who wanted to face Jane and hear her tell him she was not his mother. Liz went to see Jane first, to be sure she was the right person. Jane denied having ever seen Liz. She cursed her and told her to get off her property and not to come back.

Liz broke the news to Jerry. Jane was in fact his mother, but was in denial. Jerry believed that if he faced her, she would admit to him she was his mother. Liz drove Jerry and her mother Ruth to Georgia to see Jane again. While Jerry and Ruth remained in the car, Liz knocked on the door. Jane stepped outside and began cursing Liz and ordering her to leave. Ruth got out of the car and confronted her daughter. Jane cursed her and said she had never seen the woman before. Then Jerry got out of the car and said, "Hello, Mother." "Don't call me your mother, I never saw you before," responded Jane.

Jerry, Liz, and Ruth returned to Texas in a state of disbelief and shock. Never in his wildest nightmares did Jerry imagine his mother would not know him, or not want to see him. He was heartbroken.

A week later, Liz's phone rang. It was Jane, asking Liz to tell Jerry that she was his mother and for him to come back to see her. When Liz gave Jerry this message, his response was, "Let her come to see me, I'm not going back."

Jerry called me and told me he had accepted the fact that his mother had chosen to leave him and his siblings. He told me that he could live with what he knew now, that he did not have to worry about his mother anymore. He knew the truth and he could accept it. It was better than the unknown! He sounded like a new person, one whose burden had been lifted. Even though this did not turn out the way he dreamed, I knew he could live with what he found out.

A Brother Searches for His Brother

Dear Norma,

I last saw my older brother when I was thirteen years old, some twenty-five years ago. Matt was in the service, stationed in Korea. He came home once in 1968 and told my mother he planned to marry a Korean woman. My mother threw a fit and told him if he did, he shouldn't come back home, that she would disown him. I have not seen him since.

My other brother and sister have not seen or heard from him, either. We know he may not want any contact with us, but we want him to know we love him and care about him.

He does not know our mother died several years ago. Our grandparents have also died. Only my sister and brothers are left and we will never feel complete without Matt. I do not know whether he ever thinks of us, but he is in our thoughts.

I am enclosing Matt's date of birth, Social Security number, his service I.D. number, and the last known address I have for him.

—CHARLES

≈ ≈ ≈

Dear Charles,

Twenty-five years is a long time to wait. I under-stand how you must feel. Living without a sibling or other relative causes one to feel incomplete. Subconsciously you wonder what is going on in his life. Is he happy? Is he healthy?

I realize you and your siblings have a need to find Matt. I bet he cares very much for you, but was so hurt by your mother that he could not bear to contact anyone from home again. I'm sure he has many happy memories of you. From what you have told me, I believe Matt will be glad to hear from you and I encourage you to find him.

—NORMA

Charles could locate Matt in one day if he knew how. With a full name, date of birth, Social Security number, last known address, and a service I.D. number, almost anyone can be located!

With the name and date of birth, Charles could get Matt's driver's license by writing each state or contacting an information broker.

With the Social Security number, a letter may be forwarded by the Social Security office. Also, the Social Security number can be run through a computer database and chances are he can be located easily this way.

With the service I.D. number, Charles could check with the Veterans' Administration regional office to see if Matt has filed some type of claim.

Divorce Separates a Daughter from Her Mother

Dear Norma,

When I was five, my father returned from Vietnam and took my younger sister and me and left my mother. I never saw my mother again. I am now thirty-three years old and have always resented my father for doing this to us. I have asked him repeatedly to help me find my mother but he refuses to help. He would never allow us to visit or contact our maternal grandparents.

I have been in counseling for five years trying to learn to control my feelings of anger, hurt, and resentment toward my mother and father. I do not know whether my father abducted us or whether my mother abandoned us. I don't know who to blame or why, and I feel guilty. I have trouble trusting anyone. I live alone and I work, but I have few friends and very little interest in anything. I am in a rut and can't get out. I don't want to live the rest of my life this way.

After I severed all ties with my father when I was a teenager, he finally told me that my mother remarried and told me her new name. Apparently my mother had an affair with this man while my father was in Vietnam (he was actually a friend of my father's).

At one time my mother lived in Alabama. However, she does not appear to be there now. I have tried to contact everyone I can think of. Part of the

problem is that I do not have much information
about my mother. I know her first name is Kathy.
—LORI

~ ~ ~

Dear Lori,

The seed for the solution to your problem is your
parents' divorce. If you could obtain a copy of the
divorce record, you would have more information
about your mother. Do you have a copy of your birth
certificate? It may state your mother's correct full
name and place of birth, age, and your place of birth.
With your birth information you may request your
birth records (with a medical authorization). Once
you have her place of birth you could check there for
her birth certificate, her family, her school yearbook,
her school alumni association, death records of her
family members, and church records of her family.

Once you obtain the divorce record, you may
know some answers as to whether your mother left
your father or he left her. The reason for the divorce
may be stated.

With your mother's Social Security number,
regardless of who she is today, the Social Security
Office can identify her. If you contact Social Security,
you may be able to have a letter forwarded to your
mother for you. But you will not receive any information, other than verification of any death benefits
that might have been paid. The Internal Revenue
Service has an office of disclosure that will forward a
letter to the next of kin if he or she has filed an
income tax return.

I believe your mother can be located easily once
you get the divorce record.
—NORMA

*The parents' divorce record was located and included the mother's
Social Security number. When I entered the number into my computer, I located the mother. I contacted her by phone and she said
that her new family didn't know anything about Lori and that she
would let me know when she was ready to make contact.*

*About two weeks later, I received a call from the mother saying
she had told her family that she had two older children. It appears
that this mother left her husband and two children for another man
and made no attempt to contact the children again.*

*Eventually she met another man but did not tell him the truth
about her past. When she was contacted by Lori she seemed uncon-
cerned about Lori's problem.*

*Although Lori now knows the truth, she is having a problem
accepting it. Her mother rejected her as a five-year-old child and as a
twenty-five-year-old adult. Even in the face of the harsh reality, Lori
wants to believe her childhood fantasy, that her mother would
embrace and comfort her and tell her how much she loves her when
she found her. Isn't that what we all want?*

A Mother Looks for Her Son

Dear Norma,

My thirty-two-year-old son, Jeff, disappeared three
years ago. His car was found abandoned in the long-
term parking lot at the airport. There was no evidence of foul play. I cannot believe my son would
leave and never contact me again. The police and
other law enforcement agencies have attempted to
locate my son, but so far he has not been found.

The last person to see my son before his disappearance was his next door neighbor. According to her,
Jeff placed a garment bag in his car. Jeff had a maid
who came to his house and cleaned and did his laun-
dry. Jeff told her not to put certain clothes in his
drawer the day before he disappeared. It appears he

left of his own accord, but I do not understand why he did not tell anyone what he planned to do. I believe he would have left a note or told his brother or called me and told me he was going on a trip, but he did not.

I have another son who lived with Jeff. The two boys were very different. Jeff was the perfect gentleman, an Eagle Scout. He loved to read and was very quiet. His brother Tim was wild. Tim used drugs and alcohol and was into pornography.

I was married to the boys' father for more than twenty years before we divorced. My ex-husband came from a very wealthy family and inherited a lot of money. He died one year after Jeff disappeared. Jeff stands to inherit half of his father's fortune, which amounts to more than nine million dollars. If Jeff is not located within seven years, the money will be given to another relative. The money is currently in a trust account and I am trying to be appointed as executrix of this estate.

Can you help me find my son?
—RUTH

≈ ≈ ≈

Dear Ruth,

At first, I thought your son's disappearance might be the result of foul play. I realized that the person who had the most to gain by Jeff's disappearance was his brother Tim. With Jeff out of the way, Tim would get the entire estate.

The more I learned about Jeff, the more I became convinced that Jeff was so unhappy with his family that he probably wanted to create a new life with a new identity. Because he was very fond of adventure books, and he was an Eagle Scout, it would not surprise me to find him surviving almost anywhere.

He told the maid not to put certain clothes away, including cut-off jeans. I presume that he planned to go to a warm climate. The one thing that I could not understand was why his brother refused to talk to me. It appeared that he knew more than he was willing to tell. Whatever his reason, his behavior was strange. He refused to help me find his brother, including forbidding me to search the apartment. I did find out, however, that Jeff left his camera behind. His hobby was photography and he loved his camera. He would not have left it unless he planned to return soon. It did not appear he left for good. However, an attache case containing thousands of dollars of stock certificates was gone.

Jeff's bank account was not touched and has had no activity since his disappearance. Jeff's medical insurance was still in effect (there were no claims). Jeff's driver's license expired and was not renewed. No paper trails have been found since his disappearance.

The father's computer might contain the stock certificate information, but I was denied access to it. This case was very frustrating because your family, as a whole, was uncooperative. I did whatever I could think of, but without your cooperation, I eventually was forced to give up.

I hope that one day your family will be reunited.

—NORMA

This case took place several years ago and is still an unsolved mystery. In my opinion, the son left of his own accord to escape an unhappy family situation.

A Son Searches for His Mother

Dear Norma,

I was eleven and my brother John was nine when our father left our mother for another woman. We never saw or heard from him again. My mother struggled to support us. Times were hard, especially for a single mother. We were very poor. Our mother had to work to feed us. We were left at home alone. One day the authorities knocked on the door and took us to an orphanage. They told us that we had to live there because our mother was unable to take care of us.

Every Sunday our mother would come and take us to church and bring us candy. She would stay all afternoon, then catch a trolley and go home. We knew she loved us and that she wanted us to come back home and live with her. Unfortunately, that never happened.

Instead, my brother was sent to live with a family in Tennessee and I was sent to live with a family in Kentucky. I never saw my brother again. My name was changed. Apparently this family adopted me. I learned they paid $2,500 for me.

When I was sixteen, I ran away and returned to Nashville to find my mother. I found the house where we lived, but my mother was not there. I asked everyone, but no one knew what happened to her. I went to the police and the newspaper, but no one could find her. I never returned to the adoptive family. I lived on the streets and worked until I became an adult.

I married and had two sons of my own. As they were growing up, they asked questions about my family that I could not answer. I began searching for my brother until I found him. We kept in touch until his death several years ago. After searching for my mother for over more than sixty years, my sons decided to take over the search. They have tried very hard to find her, but so far she has not been located. I don't expect to find her alive, but I would like to know where she is buried and what became of her while she was alive. I want to know if she had other children.

My sons were able to trace my father to Texas. He died in 1949 and left his estate to his sons. Of course, no one ever notified us. But it would not have mattered, because the orphanage where my brother and I were placed stated on our records that our parents were deceased and they changed our dates of birth. We had no proof or records to show we were his sons. The estate is being held in a trust.

I am now in my eighties. My life has been consumed with the search for my mother. It looks like I will not get my answers before I die. My sons have agreed to continue the search, and their sons after them if necessary. I hope my sons eventually find all the missing pieces and will be able to claim my inheritance.

—ROBERT

≈ ≈ ≈

Dear Robert,

I researched your records at the state archives library. The books from the orphanage indicated that your birth date was changed. According to the books, your parents were deceased, which obviously was a lie. This is a very unfortunate situation. I have attempted to find a trail for your mother, but the trail ended shortly after your father left. My gut feeling is

that your mother either married or moved away.
There is no record of her death, marriage, or divorce.
She apparently was employed and was listed in several of the old directories. I found a record of her
brother also. The family cemetery is located in
another county. I believe a county historian or even
church records may be located.

    I'm sorry your search lasted your entire lifetime. I
wish I could have helped more.
—NORMA

With a search like this, an information broker may be necessary.
They will be able to search a database for missing persons using only
a first name or approximate year of birth.

7

Finding Your Father

ALTHOUGH I'M not a psychologist, after many years of working with searchers, I've learned that there is a deep psychological need for every child to know his or her birth parents. No matter why the father is absent, his children need to know his identity. They yearn for a role model. They want security and long for love. They wish their father could provide those basic needs and they dream of a long-lost relationship. But even if they will not have those needs fulfilled, mere knowledge about their father will provide the identity that is so vital to human development.

Dear Norma,

My mother came from a very dysfunctional family. She grew up without feeling loved or wanted. She longed for someone to care about her. At age sixteen she got in some minor trouble and was placed temporarily in a juvenile detention home. A counselor was assigned to her. The counselor told my mother that she needed someone to care for and love, that someday she should have a baby, that it would probably be the best thing she could do.

Eventually, my mother left home and went to visit relatives in Nebraska. She met a nice man, Bill, who was older and going through a divorce. Bill was the father of three beautiful daughters. This man was very kind to my mother. My mother thought it would be wonderful to have a baby, someone to love and care for. Bill had beautiful turquoise eyes and my mother thought she would like to have a daughter with this man's eyes. My mother became pregnant, but never told Bill. In fact, she never saw him again after she learned she was pregnant. She moved away and had me.

While I was very small, my mother married and I was raised by a wonderful stepfather, whom I adore. I learned about Bill when I was a teenager. Of course I became very curious and wondered what Bill was like. My mother told me the whole story so I knew I had three stepsisters.

I am now twenty-four years old and I think it is time I found my father and met my stepsisters. Because none of them know I exist, I do not know how to approach them or how to handle the situation so that I do not hurt anyone.
—JENNIFER

≈ ≈ ≈

Dear Jennifer,

Because no one had been told about you, this news could create a major problem for your father if it is not handled properly. Finding people is an awesome responsibility. The approach must be carefully planned and executed. Regardless of what we find, I know you need to find your father and that you have no intention of causing him a problem. I'm sure he will be very proud of you.

Your mother was very young and knew only your father's name and the place he lived when she met him. She knew he was going through a divorce and she had seen his children.

Based on this information I believe the seed for your solution is his divorce record, where we should find his date of birth, and possibly his Social Security number, his employer at the time of the divorce, and his last known address. With this information, he should be located easily with a search for his name, his driver's license, and any vehicles registered to him. Neighbors at his last known address, his former employer, and even his ex-wife probably know his whereabouts. He probably paid child support. Perhaps he still visits his children. Their names should also be on the divorce record, along with that of his ex-wife. All of them may still be in the same state as they were at the time of the divorce. Many people remain within one hundred miles of where they were born and raised.

All the best,
—NORMA

Bill was found. When Jennifer's mother sent him a photograph of his daughter, he was surprised, but delighted. The resemblance between Jennifer and Bill's youngest daughter by his former wife was amazing. Yes, Jennifer has the most beautiful turquoise eyes, just like her father's. Jennifer met her father and her three stepsisters for the first time on television. It was wonderful.

The Most Common Search of All

The most requested search I receive is from adults who never knew their fathers. They either do not know who he is or the parents divorced when the child was young and the father has not been heard from since.

> *Fifty percent of all chilren are raised by a single parent (predominantly the mother), and fifty percent of those children never know the absent parent (usually the father).*

Reasons fathers are absent include: unwed mothers (approximately 3,500 babies are born out of wedlock every day in the United States); divorce (approximately 3,000 couples divorce every day in the United States); teenage pregnancies; father in military; and/or father unaware of the child's existence.

Living with the Unknown

I've learned from my clients that one of the worst tragedies in life is living with the unknown and suppressing the desire to know. Searchers secretly ask:

Who is my father?
Does he love me?
Does he know I exist?
Do I look like him?
Would he be proud of me?
What is my medical background?
Where did my father's ancestors originate?
Do I have brothers and sisters?
Do I have grandparents?
Would my other family members want to meet me?

Unfortunately, children who live with the unknown fantasize about what they suppress. If they don't know their fathers, they may pretend that their fathers are famous and therefore simply "too busy" for their children. They imagine that they are like their fathers and have talent for something (like ball playing) because their fathers are professionals of some sort. "I'm a good football player because my daddy is a pro," a child might say about his absent father.

Suppressing the desire to know one's father may cause psychological damage that appears in the form of behavioral problems. Children or teenagers are not necessarily bad but sometimes are crying for help. Failure to understand fatherless children's real difficulties may cause additional problems. This may lead to other complications such as criminal behavior.

In Search of Role Models

Nature intended for children to have two parents, and children have specific needs that only a father or a mother can meet, in each one's special ways. When these needs aren't met, development is thwarted and psychological damage may result. Children who have no contact with a missing parent may develop an inability to function normally as adults or to be good parents.

Children who do not have positive role models often do not become positive role models for their own children. Children of absent parents become insecure and have low self-esteem. When they become adults, they realize that for their lives to be "normal" or complete, they must know who their father is. They must find him in order to release their fears and anger.

Cries for Help

Adults searching for a father are not necessarily expecting a relationship with him, although most will hope for a friendship. The search is not meant to cause the father embarrassment, to hurt him, or to seek material gain. Its interest is to allow the child to put his or her need to rest. Once children have information about their fathers, discovering who he is, where he is, what he is like, they can go on with their lives.

The search for a father is a search for the unknown. Regardless of what the child finds, it is better than not knowing. Denying a child the right to information about a father is a form of victimization. The child becomes an innocent victim, and victims need help.

I receive thousands of letters and phone calls from people who want and need to find their fathers. I consider these requests cries for help. I understand the need, and I've learned that understanding is comforting to those searching for a loved one. Knowing that someone understands, is willing to help, and will try to make life better offers them hope and is spiritually uplifting. Finding a loved one, especially a father or mother, is a form of healing—it mends broken hearts.

Getting the Basic Facts Together

To search for your father, it is best to know his name. Only your birth mother, your birth certificate, your parents' divorce documents, or a cooperative relative can provide this information.

Once you have a name to look for, you may find other information or clues, such as what state your father was born in, what type of employment he had, where he lived at the time of your birth, and what school he attended.

Bear in mind that it is easier to find someone with an unusual name than with a common one. Also, it is not unusual for someone to change the spelling of his or her name—"i" may be changed to "e," for example, or "e" to "y."

Begin with whatever information is known. The more information, the better the chances of finding the father.

The four pieces of information that will make the search the easiest are: full correct name; last known address; date of birth; and Social Security number.

If the searcher has these four pieces of information, I can almost guarantee that the father will be found, unless he is deliberately hiding, he is in a government protection program, he is in another country, or he is deceased and his body has not been found.

Tips for Father Searchers

Here are some tips for finding your father:

1. Obtain a copy of your birth certificate.
2. Obtain copies of all your birth medical records.
3. Obtain a copy of your parents' divorce documents, if possible.
4. Assemble on paper all known information, and list all possible places to search. Each piece of information is a clue that should lead to another piece of information. With a name only, a search may begin in a library, courthouse, or on the Internet.
5. Search the Internet for a phone number (www.yahoo.com/search/people) or e-mail address (www.four11.com).
6. Register with an on-line registry (www.findme.org).

A reference librarian can show you how to browse the Internet, can suggest available search materials and techniques and possibly direct you to volunteer searchers, genealogists, historians, or other interested parties who can assist you (there may be fees involved). Of course, you also have the option of hiring a private investigator. Public records at a local city hall, courthouse, and state or federal government office may be obtained by written request. Consider sending letters to:

- the last known address, with "Address Correction Requested" written on the envelope;
- Social Security, 6401 Security Blvd., Baltimore, MD 21235, with a request that they forward a letter to your father for "humanitarian purposes";
- the IRS "Office of Disclosure," to forward the enclosed letter to your father. (The "humanitarian purposes" rule applies and you must be the next of kin.);
- the National Personnel Records Center, 9700 Page Blvd., St. Louis, MO 63132;
- a state Office of War Records to verify dates of service of enlistment or discharge;

- the county courthouse of father's birth county for a copy of his birth certificate; and/or
- a Veterans' Administration office, which may have a military veteran's claim (claim number is the service I.D. number or the Social Security number).

Ten More Steps in the Right Direction

Depending on the information you have, you should also do the following:

1. Search on-line (www.ancestry.com/ssdi) for death records for members of your father's family. Obtaining a date of death of a grandparent or relative will lead to an obituary that may contain a list of survivors. This may also lead to probate records for a will or settlement of an estate.

2. Check for school records or yearbooks.

3. Consult census records.

4. Check for driver's license and vehicle, property, and voter's registration. (Driver's license and voter's record usually require a name and date of birth.)

5. Check for lawsuits, judgments, liens, and bankruptcies in case he owes money.

6. Check for traffic tickets and criminal histories.

7. Check membership directories for civic organizations or associations.

8. Check professional licensing.

9. Check with a county historian for possible family cemeteries. A small town's historian is usually a great person to ask for help.

10. Check for a divorce; he may have married several times.

Beware of Fantasies

It is vital for you, as an adult searcher, to be prepared for what you may find. Those who have spent their lives fantasizing (a form of denial) about what great guys their fathers are, and how glad they will be to hear from them, often do not foresee rejection or disappointment. Searchers need to be prepared to accept the truth and to understand that whatever they find is better than the alternative—the unknown.

8

Looking for Your Mother

TRYING TO find your mother can be one of the most com-
pelling and traumatic efforts imaginable. Because women are
likely to change their names when married, this search can be
more difficult than looking for fathers. And considering the fact
that your mother is actually the one who gave you life, some
would say looking for your mother involves more emotional risk
as well.

Four facts—seeds of information—will help enormously: the
mother's maiden name; where she was born; where she gave
birth; and where she lived when the child was born (in addition
to the standard information of last known address, date of birth,
and Social Security number).

Dear Norma,

I need your help. I'm looking for my birth mother.
I'm twenty-four years old and I was a foster child,
along with my sister. We went to a nice family when I
was about three or four years old. Through the years,
until I was about twelve or thirteen, my birth mother
kept in touch, calling me about once a week. I lived
in Connecticut (all my life) and she lived in Texas

then. I had not heard from her for about ten or eleven years until last year on my birthday. I had a message from her on my answering machine saying that she loves me and misses me. (She said the reason I stopped hearing from her was because my foster mother and the Department of Children and Youth Services told her to stop because I missed her and it was making me upset.)

I'm getting married soon and I want my birth mother to be there. I still love her and my dream is to find her. Please, can you help me or send information on how I can find her? My name is Dawn and I'm in Bridgeford, Connecticut. My birth mother's maiden and married names are Hailey and Stevens.

Thank you.

—DAWN

Finding a Paper Trail

In most states, adopted people can obtain their own birth records (with a medical authorization). Once you've obtained your birth record, you have your mother's name, possibly her date of birth and/or a Social Security number, an address at the time she gave birth, and her physician and insurance carrier. For an adoptee looking for a birth mother, the seed for the search is the birth record. If you were separated from your mother because of a marital separation or divorce, the steps to finding her are different. Usually the mother raises the children. If this was not true in your case, a divorce record is the most useful document.

When a child is abandoned, there is usually very little to go on because there are no trails to follow. Only rarely is any sort of document available. These are difficult searches—practically impossible—unless there is some kind of information.

Sources of Information

The most important thing in a mother search is to begin with the correct name. It's not unusual for someone along the way to provide a wrong name, leading to a eventual dead end. Make sure the spelling is right. If the searcher is around sixty years old and the mother is about eighty, the census records may be the most helpful source of information. The most recent records that have been released are from the 1920 census. However, if you are next of kin, you don't have to wait for another census to be released. You can receive information now from the census bureau.

Making the Right Approach

Just as men and women have fantasies about their fathers, they also have them about their mothers. It's important for searchers to hope for the best. But be prepared for the worst when actually making contact.

Careful preparation must be made. This may be a one-shot opportunity; if it is not handled properly, it can be a disaster. The situation may well be irreversible if it is not handled wisely. A life can be ruined and a chance at a relationship destroyed.

Try to put yourself in the mother's shoes. If someone knocked on your door and didn't explain properly what the visit was about, emotions could prove to be overwhelming. Fears may surface, wounds may be opened, and regret and guilt may erupt after having long been suppressed. The mother may be in a state of denial, unprepared for a reunion. Negative emotions are especially possible if rape or other traumatic experience was involved. An abrupt confrontation with a birth mother can cause emotional and psychological problems, even though the searcher did not intend to cause any harm.

The pros and cons of approaching a birth mother must be weighed carefully before any action is taken. I recommend that a third party make the approach, someone who is not involved emotionally, preferably someone who has experience at this sort of thing. Search and support groups are available in almost every city, and many provide free services. You can access many search and support groups on the Internet. One such support group is Halcyon Adoption Support (mmci.tallynet.com) that allows you to talk to other people who have experienced much of the same difficulties that such searches cause. These people can offer opinions and advice, or they can suggest an experienced third-party intermediary. Otherwise, a minister or therapist may be the best person to reach out and prepare the way. Regardless of who makes the approach, it should be nonthreatening.

Approaching a birth mother requires compassion for her feelings, consideration of her current status, and most of all, courage. Do not do this yourself. Get help from a third party, preferably a professional.

Tips for Mother Searchers

Here are some tips for finding your mother:

1. Learn her maiden name.
2. Estimate her age.
3. Learn her date of birth.
4. Discover her place of birth.
5. Find out her last known address.
6. Look for school records and yearbooks.
7. Search for church directories and baptismal records.
8. Get birth certificates—yours and hers.
9. Try to find death records of family members. Check the Social Security Death Index at www.ancestry.com/ssdi.
10. Seek your birth medical records.
11. Search the Internet for a phone number (www.yahoo.com/search/people) or e-mail address (www.four11.com).

12. Register with an on-line registry (www.findme.org).
13. Check out the reference library's crisscross directory for the years before and after your birth for all families with her last name.
14. Talk to neighbors, current residents, mail carrier, community historian, the town "busybody," teachers, and social workers.
15. While searching, avoid using the word adoption. Substitute *family tree* or *genealogy*.

In Search of a Mended Heart

The search for a mother is a search for a mended heart. One letter from a woman who wanted to find out if her mother was still alive stands out in my memory as one of the most touching I have ever received. It was written to a local television station after I appeared on a show that featured a mother-daughter reunion. Let me share it with you.

Dear Channel 4,

About four to six weeks ago, I was watching your program and you had a lady on your show who united a mother and daughter who had not seen each other in many years. I did not write down the address but would like to search for my mother and half-brother. I have not seen my mother since approximately 1946, but I did receive a letter in 1950 that was not given to me until after my father's death. I do not believe my mother is alive. She was born in April 1909. Enclosed is all the information I have.

Please forward this letter or write and let me know the address of this lady. Maybe she can help me.
—Teresa

Here is the letter Teresa had received from her mother in 1950:

Dearest Teresa and Dawn,

I guess after these many years of not writing I will drop you a line and let you know I still love you and haven't forgotten you kids for one minute of the day. Hope that you are both okay and getting along well in school.

I am remarried again and he is in the army. I have been married to Howard for almost three years. I am very happy and he is really very good to me. You should see your little brother that we have. He is almost two years old. He was born [she provided dates and the name of the hospital in Battle Creek, Michigan]. His name is John. He sure is a good boy and is as sweet as he can be. Howard really loves him.

What grade are you kids in now? What school do you go to? How is Grandpa? How is your new stepmother? I hope she is good to you.

Battle Creek is a real nice town. It isn't as large as one would think with all the factories they have here. We don't live too far away from the Kellogg and Post factories that make Corn Flakes and all kinds of cereals.

There isn't any snow at all but I have heard over the radio that you have had plenty of snow and cold weather. The winter here is very mild and has been all year.

Well, Teresa, you will be fourteen years old.

I hope you are a good girl. Please send me a picture of you and Dawn. I'll send you a picture of John as soon as I get to town to have some taken.

Write me real soon and let me know all the news, that is, if your dad will let you write. I imagine he has really turned you kids against me. I'll write again if you let me know where you are. I am sending this to the old address.

Love to you both,

—YOUR MOTHER.

9

Adoption: The Decision of a Lifetime

THE ADOPTION search is a trying one, but it can result in some very satisfying reunions. Here's an overview of the adoption process:

Birth mother makes decision to allow baby to be adopted.
Birth mother may enter a home for unwed mothers.
Birth mother chooses a private or public agency to handle the adoption.
Birth mother has baby.
　　Birth mother's medical records completed.
　　Child's medical records prepared.
　　Child's original birth certificate issued.
　　Birth mother signs surrender of parental rights after baby's birth. Depending on the year and court of jurisdiction, the birth mother may have two weeks to one year to change her mind.

Agency takes baby from hospital to either a foster home or the adoptive family's home. Agency may provide "home studies."

Child is placed in adoptive family's home. Adoptive family hires attorney to handle adoption proceedings.

Attorney files a petition for adoption with the court of jurisdiction, usually after the surrender is final (two weeks to two years from date of birth).

Usually one year from the time the petition for adoption is filed, a final decree of adoption is issued by the court.

An amended birth certificate with the child's new name is issued.

Records are sealed and sent to the Office of Vital Statistics.

In actuality, there are several different types of adoptions. Some are done through a public agency such as a state Department of Human Services. Some are done through private agencies that are usually connected with religious denominations. Some are independent or private adoptions handled through a doctor or a lawyer. In some instances, these professionals' family members are given a child to raise and the mother disappears. Unfortunately, some adoptions are illegal and are the result of black market and gray market activities. Some are run by greedy private agencies that care only about money and actually sell children. If an illegal adoption took place, the paper trail is probably nonexistent or false.

Every person involved in the adoption process has a collection of fears: of each other, about their pasts, and about their futures. As always, the most overwhelming fear is the fear of the unknown.

Here are three myths about the key players in adoptions: adoptees remain children forever and are never capable of making decisions as to what is in their best interest; the adoptive family's relationship with the adopted child will not endure if the child meets a member of his or her biological family; and, biological parents are irresponsible and immature and will remain so for the rest of their lives.

Cast those falsehoods aside, and as you begin your adoption search, keep these guidelines in mind:

- Know the rules of the game: state laws. Read the adoption laws for the current year and the year of the adoption. Request identifying information from the state Department of Human Services. Obtain public records from the court of jurisdiction if available (petition/final decree). Obtain court order to have sealed adoption records opened by the court of jurisdiction. Obtain medical records at birth, with medical authorization. Obtain copy of original birth certificate. Everyone involved in the search needs to write the state a letter waiving his or her confidentiality and requesting that he or she receive any letters from anyone who might be searching for him or her. Consider registering in a missing person's registry.

- Know the players: adoptees, birth parents, adoptive parents. Contact adoption agency and attorneys.

- Know what it takes to win: Learn how to conduct a successful search, how to approach the person you are looking for, and how to prepare for the reunion.

- Play fair: Don't obtain information illegally, and don't lie, cheat, or steal when obtaining information. Respect the feelings of all those involved. Don't disrupt their lives, do harm, or cause trouble.

Special Provisions for Native Americans

The Indian Child Welfare Act of 1978 (Public Law 95-608) entitles adoptees of Native American heritage, including Eskimos and Aleuts, to special rights.

Native American Adoptees also retain their rights of inheritance. Section 301(b) reads: "Upon the request of the adopted Indian child over the age of eighteen, the adoptive or foster parents of an Indian child, or an Indian tribe, the Secretary of the Interior shall disclose such information as may be necessary for the enrollment of an Indian child in the tribe in which the child may be eligible for enrollment for determining any right or benefits associated with that membership."

Birth Parents Looking for Their Children

Let me warn you that when it comes to searching for your child, you will probably not receive a lot of sympathy from anyone. There is a slim chance that one of three people might be willing to help you: the social worker who assisted you at the time of adoption; the attending physician; or the attorney who processed the adoption paperwork.

Birth parents usually don't understand the adoption procedure beyond the point of surrender. They are not aware of the process the adoptive family went through to get the child. They do not know what records exist, where the records are housed, how to ask questions, or how to begin. They are usually told that the records are sealed and that they have no rights. The only thing that most birth parents know is that they had a baby and signed a paper.

Dear Norma,

I was an unwed mother at the age of seventeen. I came from a very good family. I fell in love with my boyfriend and I became pregnant just before he was sent overseas. He told me we would marry when he returned. My parents were very ashamed of me. They made arrangements for me to go to another city and stay at a home for unwed mothers. They did not want anyone to know I was pregnant. In 1955, an unwed mother was considered "trash." Although I was ashamed, embarrassed, and humiliated, I did not feel like a bad person. I was frightened about having a baby. I did not know what to expect. Arrangements were made for my baby to be adopted. I was given no options. My parents would not hear of my keeping the baby. I could not raise a baby, I did not know how to support myself. My boyfriend knew I was pregnant, but he was unprepared for the responsibility of a family. I felt that I had no options.

Even though I wanted my baby, I wanted to do what was best for her. I was brainwashed into believing that my baby would have a better chance with a family that could give her all the things she would need. Allowing my baby to be adopted was supposed to be in the best interests of my baby. I never even thought that my choice to allow my baby to be adopted was anything other than an act of love. I loved her and wanted her to have all the things I could not provide. She needed a mother and a father, a secure, stable family that would take good care of her. Giving my baby up was out of love, not because I did not want her. My daughter is now thirty years old. Every year on her birthday I cry all day and wonder where she is, who she is, and if her adoptive family loves her as much as I do. I only saw her for a short time, but I will never forget her. I wonder if she ever thinks of me, if she hates me for not keeping her. I have lived with guilt and regret for thirty long years. I eventually married another man. We had three other children. I have told them they have an older sister and they also want me to find her. My life will always be incomplete and I will always have a place in my heart for my first daughter. I want her to know how much I love her.
—BETTY

Dear Betty,

I have heard similar stories from almost every birth mother who has ever contacted me. There is a pattern to all the requests I receive. I almost know before a birth mother tells me exactly what she is about to say about the hurt, the guilt, and the regret. I know that being an unwed mother is very difficult, both mentally and emotionally.

After talking to hundreds of birth mothers, I think I understand how they feel and the reasons for their searches. I realize that they have no intention of taking their biological child away from the adoptive family. (In fact, I have never met a birth mother who intended to do that.) It appears to me that there is a lot of misunderstanding about adoptees and biological families searching for each other. I see a need for an educational process to take place in which adoptive families understand the need for adoptees to know their identities in order to develop normally. If denied their identity, adoptees may have problems dealing with the unknown.

I know you need to find your daughter.

—NORMA

I found Betty's daughter. She had been adopted by a doctor who worked at the hospital where she was born. The daughter was thrilled to know her mother was looking for her. She had always wanted to know her biological mother and had always thought of her on her birthday. For fear of hurting her adoptive parents, she had not begun her search, although she had planned to do so without telling the adoptive parents. Once I contacted her, she could not wait to meet her mother and her other siblings. The meeting was wonderful. Betty has also visited Sandra and met her three grandchildren. Sandra felt the need to tell her adoptive parents about finding her birth mother. The adoptive family was not upset, especially when Sandra reassured them that they were always going to be her parents. She wanted them to meet her biological mother so they would know that they had

nothing to fear. The relationship has filled a void in their lives, allow-ing all of them to feel complete and rid themselves of the unknown.

From my perspective, giving up a child for adoption is the ultimate act of love. A birth mother has to sign a surrender ter-minating her maternal rights forever when she makes the choice to put her child up for adoption. This mother gives up her own flesh and blood, not because she doesn't love or want the baby, but because she loves it so much.

Often in the past, birth mothers were not given options. Usually their parents made their decision for them, especially if they were underage. A young girl who gave up a baby may have lived with regret and guilt, made a thousand times worse by knowing that she had no rights to inquire about her child again.

Dear Norma,

During my sophomore year of college I became a father. I had dated Brenda for four years. We both came from wonderful families; in fact, our families were old friends. I had known her since early child-hood. She was a cheerleader at another college. Because we were not at the same school, we did not see each other often. I did not know Brenda was preg-nant until about the fifth month. By then, her family had arranged for her to "visit Aunt Ruth." When I learned she was pregnant, I was sure it was mine and I wanted to marry her and raise our child.

Pressure from her family and not being ready for the responsibility led Brenda to give the child up for adoption. I was against this but was not allowed to be a part of the decision. I offered to pay medical expenses and do whatever I could. I felt so guilty and responsible. I was hurt and angry because Brenda would not marry me or allow me to have anything to do with this decision. I had no rights, no say-so about the future of my son.

For twenty-one long years I have lived with guilt and regret. Even though I eventually married someone else and had other children, not a day goes by that I don't think about my first son and wonder if he has a loving adoptive family. I worry that he is abused or needs me for something. I cannot bear to live without knowing who my son is and if he is okay. I need to know he has a good family that can provide for him. If he needs anything, I want to give him whatever I can. I want him to know I have always cared, that he has been in my thoughts since he was born. I need to find my son.

—KEN

≈ ≈ ≈

Dear Ken,

Finding a child who was adopted involves much more than you may realize. After a successful search, which may be difficult, there must come planning, preparing, and counseling with you and your son. You don't just go find someone and appear in his life. Locating an adoptee is an awesome responsibility. Consideration must be taken not to disrupt anyone's life and not to create a problem for the adoptee or his family. Careful planning and preparation are essential.

Because you have initiated this search, I recommend you talk to the biological mother to see if she would like to find her son. She can provide you with the names of the hospital, doctor, the city and state of birth, and the adoption agency she chose to place the baby.

All of this information is very important. Each piece of information is like a piece of a puzzle, so the more pieces you have to work with, the easier it is to complete the puzzle. Once you have talked to her I will go to the courthouse (where the seed for the solution rests) in the city in which she relinquished the baby.
—NORMA

Brenda (who had remarried) said she feared that her new husband might not understand about the son she gave up for adoption. Although Brenda did not want to find her son, she understood and supported Ken's search. She provided the basic information, as well as the baby's original name. She even offered to try to obtain a copy of his original birth certificate.

With the information provided by Brenda, the search began at the courthouse of a small town. Looking through the docket appearance books for the eighteen months after the baby was born, I found that ten families had adopted sons and only one had the birthdate provided by Brenda.

In a nearby town, I found the son, David, working in his uncle's store. I told him I was a private investigator working on a case in the area. He was friendly and easy to talk to. I visited the store twice a week and we became friends. He told me about his girlfriend, who had been adopted and was searching for her birth mother. This was my chance to ask if he too was adopted. "Yes," he said, although he was not searching for his birth parents. "I don't have any desire to find them," he said. "I don't believe they would be people I would be proud of."

I asked him why. His adoptive parents had told him his father was in the navy; therefore he concluded that the father probably was on furlough when he impregnated a prostitute. David thought he would be ashamed of his father.

"Would you want to meet your father if he is someone you would be proud of?" I asked.

"Yes," he said. "If my biological parents are not people I would be ashamed of, I might want to know who they are."

During our next visit I told David that I thought I knew who his father was, and that David would be proud of him. "He comes from a fine family, is well educated, has a good job, and is very successful."

David's face lit up. It was the most encouraging thing he had ever heard about his biological family.

"If you ever decide you want to know who your biological father is, I will tell you," I said.

The next week David said, "I've thought about what you said about meeting my birth father," he said. "I want to meet him."

The father was grateful to me for finding his son, and it resulted in a successful meeting. The two of them have become friends, all the while giving careful consideration to the adoptive family. The birth father wanted to know his son, and not hurt the adoptive family, for he was grateful to them for raising the son he could never forget.

Write a Letter to Your Child

No one may have told you this: you can write to the agency that handles adoption in the state of your child's birth, waiving your rights to confidentiality. This authorizes the state to release information about you if your child inquires. You may also write a letter to your child, and if the child is trying to locate you, the letter may be given to him or her.

It is disappointing, often devastating, to the adoptee who inquires when he or she comes of age, to find that no letter is waiting. Their already established sense of rejection is only intensified.

A Matter of Public Record

One thing you'll want to do first is to see what the law says about adoption in the state where your child was born. More than likely, the adoptive family went to a judge, had an attorney, and filed with an agency—all before the birth occurred. The court probably gave a trial period of one year before the adoption was final. This means there's a paper trail. You can get help from a reference librarian at the public library or go to the Internet. The Internet is full of resources to help adoptees and/or birth parents find each other. At the Website www.states.org you can find out the different adoption laws by state. You can also search a search engine such as Alta Vista (www.altavista.digital.com) or Infosee (www.infoseek.com) to find Websites that will be helpful.

Were the records public? Is the court responsible for maintaining a daily log? Yes. There should be a book somewhere documenting everybody who appears in court. Although it is not made public in every state, in many states it is public information. This docket appearance book records who appeared in the local county courthouse, the date, and the reason for the appearance.

There may be separate books specifically regarding adoptions, just as there may be separate books for divorces, wills, and other civil issues. Usually only one court in the courthouse handles adoptions. Find out which one it is.

The search for an adoptee begins with the paper trail at the courthouse. Look at the appropriate time frame in the docket appearance book (if it is a public record) for all children who were adopted through the placing agency that you used. Process of elimination will narrow the possibility of which child is yours by sex of the child, the adoptive agency, and other specific facts.

Your chances of finding your child are better if you went through a private agency rather than a public one. A private agency may handle only a dozen male and a dozen female adoptions in the adoptee's county of birth per year.

My advice is never to use the word *adoption* when dealing with county clerks. Substitute the phrases *family tree* or *genealogical* research.

Thanks to modern technology, there is an alternative to following paper trails. Now you can sign onto a missing persons registry that will match up two people who are searching for each other if there is mutual consent. Both parties must be registered. There are many mutual consent reunion registries on the Internet. Most operate at no cost to the registrant; some ask for a donation; others charge a fee to registrants to have information entered into a database. I operate such a registry, which I call Reu-Net, the International Missing Persons Registry. The computer does the work for you. It is capable of matching two people who are both registered whenever certain information matches, such as a date of birth, hospital, agency, or place of birth. (At the time of writing this book the registration fee is only $20 for one year.) To register your search in Reu-Net (an acronym for Reunion Network), go to www.reunion.copm; or to receive a registration form and brochure about this service, send a self-addressed stamped envelope to: Reu-Net, P.O. Box 210333, Nashville, TN 37229-0333. You may also place a personal message or classified ad to your missing person in my on-line Missing Persons Magazine, also at www.reunion.com.

At www.reunion.com you may link to many other registries, searchable databases, search and support groups, and other informational sites of interest. At these on-line registries, you can search the database to see if anyone is searching for you. You can also register your information via forms on-line. if you're looking for support or need new ideas about your information, there are a large number of resources available, including e-mail support lists, listings of support groups all over the United States, and chat rooms.

In order to take advantage of many of the chat rooms available to those touched by adoption, you will need to download an IRC Client. IRC stands for Internet Relay Chat. I highly recommend the IRC Client mIRCv5.x available at www.mirc.com/ or www.mirc.co.uk/ as shareware.

Once downloaded, installed, and setup, your IRC Client

can open up worlds of information to you. IRC enables you to chat in 'real time' with other people. Internet Relay Chat has many servers, such as DALnet (www.dal.net/), FEFnet (www.fef.net/) and others. DALnet has several adoption related chat channels (or rooms) available. If you have questions about IRC or mIRC and how to use it, there are great tutorials on the Web to teach you how to use them.

No Surprises, Please!

It is vital that the birth parent understands the importance of the approach to the birth child. Even though the intent is not to disrupt the child or the adoptive family, unpleasant or even traumatic situations can happen if the approach is not handled properly.

One woman, for instance, wanted to contact her daughter on her eighteenth birthday. This "surprise gift" was a shock both to the girl and to her adoptive mother. Because the girl dearly loved her adoptive mother, who was extremely upset by the news, the daughter turned against her birth mother.

This birthday surprise was a total disaster. The girl has never spoken to her birth mother again. The birth mother may never have a second chance because her approach was inappropriate and ill-advised.

A third party is invaluable at this sensitive stage. An experienced private investigator, a search group or organization, a minister, or a therapist with experience in this type of work is preferable to an emotional family member or a blundering friend, however well-intentioned they may be.

Fearing the Unknown

There are many fears and myths associated with adoption. The adoptee fears rejection by birth parents. He may also fear discovering that his parents were criminal, insane, or otherwise objectionable or undesirable individuals. In addition, there is a concern about receiving bad medical news, such as a family congenital condition or a predisposition toward cancer or heart disease.

Adoptees are reluctant to cause pain to their adoptive families by searching for birth parents, thinking that such a search implies that the adoptive family "didn't love enough" or "didn't do a good job." Adoptees may experience "guilt trips" for asking questions about their biological families. Adoptees have a normal, natural curiosity about their identities.

The adoptive family fears losing the love of the adopted child or having an undesirable person suddenly enter their lives. They secretly suspect that they haven't lived up to their adopted child's expectations and feel wounded because they've tried hard to be good parents.

The birth parent fears rejection by the child, who may be embittered because of the adoption or who feels abandoned. Birth parents may also fear financial complications or that past indiscretions such as unwed parenthood will be revealed to their spouses and children. Often the birth parent blocks the painful memory of relinquishing a child for adoption.

> *Searching for birth relatives is not an insult to adoptive families.*

Looking for Birth Parents

Just as birth parents searching for their children don't receive much sympathy, adoptees searching for their birth parents, although they may receive sympathy, don't receive much help. First, examine the information you know about yourself: adoptive name, adoptive parents, date of birth, city and state of birth, placing agency, and city and state in which the adoption took place.

Most people are able to begin their adoption search by contacting the agency or lawyer that handled the adoption in order to request identifying information. However, in Kansas and Alaska, records are open to adoptees at the age of majority. In these two states, adoptees are given all of the identifying information in their file. Most states, when a request of identifying information is requested, a petition to open the adoption record is then filed. Some will send nonidentifying information. Nonidentifying information is information about the birth family or adoptive family that does not include names, addresses, or phone numbers of the individuals.

Dear Norma,

I am a thirty-seven-year-old married mother of two grown children. I am a registered nurse. I was adopted at birth and have wanted to know about my biological family all my life. I was never very compatible with my adoptive family. My adoptive mother has refused to tell me anything about my adoption. I actively began my search for my biological family ten years ago, but have not made much progress.

You were referred to me by a mutual acquaintance. I understand you have found many birth families, as well as many adoptees. When I contacted you, you were kind enough to explain the adoption process to me and you also referred me to an attorney who has been very successful at having adoption records opened by court order.

I took your advice and contacted this attorney. Once the petition to have my records opened was filed by the attorney, the judge allowed me to have my records opened. Not only was I able to view my sealed adoption records, I was able to find my birth mother.

I decided that I wanted to contact her by phone. When I called she immediately asked if I was her daughter. She explained that she had searched for me until about ten years ago. She had given up on ever finding me. We were reunited immediately. My birth mother had married someone other than my father and she had two sons by this marriage. She wanted me to meet her husband and my two half-brothers. It was wonderful to finally know who I looked like and have answers to all the questions I had always wanted to know. Most of all, it was wonderful to know that my mother loved me and cared about me. Having her put her arms around me and embrace me was the most comforting feeling I have ever known.

Not only did I meet my mother, but we also became the best of friends. We both had felt a void all these years and we wanted to heal all the hurt and pain from being separated. My mother told me that she never wanted to give me up, that she was young and unwed. My grandmother made all the arrangements for my adoption. My mother was never given any options. She was told by her mother that she could not keep me. In fact, my grandmother arranged for her hair stylist to adopt me. It was a private adoption. My grandmother always knew who had me, where I was, and who I was. In fact, she continued to be a customer in my adoptive mother's beauty salon and watched me grow up without ever letting me know who she was. My adoptive mother always knew who my mother was and would never tell me anything.

My birth mother told me she loved me and wanted to keep me and had grieved for me all these years. My grandmother would never tell her who adopted me. Once we shared our life stories, we realized that we were separated because my grandmother thought it was best, not because my mother chose to give me up. All these years I have been so unhappy and have longed to know the circumstances of my adoption, yet even though my adoptive mother knew everything, she refused to tell me anything. Because of this, I do not plan to be around her again. She made my life miserable.

Finding my birth mother has made me feel complete. I know the story of my adoption, who my father is, and that I have siblings. I'm sure not many people realize how important this is to an adoptee. I'm sure not many adoptees would feel the resentment toward their adoptive family as I do. If my adoptive mother could have understood how important this void was and what it would have meant to me for her to tell me the truth, I would probably not feel so badly toward her now.

Once I met my birth mother and found that she and I are so much alike, I became very close to her and we love each other very much. My birth mother and I agreed that we wanted to begin our relationship again.

—B.N.

❧ ❧ ❧

Dear B.N.,

I have kept in touch with you to see how things are going, and you have told me what an emotional roller coaster this has been. It sounds like you need to have some professional counseling because you still seem very angry and bitter. This can be emotionally draining and you need to release these feelings. Your emptiness and void are gone. You know the truth.

You don't have to live with the unknown anymore. You must let go of the hurt. You need to accept the fact that you cannot change the past and you need to go on with the present and future. You can live with what you know; it's what you did not know that was actually causing the problem.

Searching for a birth parent requires a lot of preparation and you did not have this. You were not ready emotionally for the consequences. It sounds like you may have a touch of guilt about the bitterness toward your adoptive family and anger toward your grandmother.

It has occurred to me that at the time your mother was pregnant, your grandmother thought she was doing what was in your best interest and your mother's best interest, and she loved you enough to want you to be raised by someone she knew and trusted. She apparently did not want a stranger to have you and she was able to monitor your childhood at a distance.

—NORMA

Finding her birth mother has made a difference in B.N.'s life, but she is not completely happy. I think adoptees need to be told about their biological families at an early age. It's too bad no one ever told her adoptive family how damaging it was to not tell her the truth about her birth family. I think laws should be passed making it mandatory for an adoptive family to be counseled concerning the adoptee's need to know his or her identity in order to develop normally.

Write to the state Department of Human Services, Adoption Services, authorizing release of identifying information about yourself and requesting identifying information about your birth parents. (This request is referred to as a Waiver of Confidentiality/Request for Identifying Information.)

Include all of the information you have about your adoption, as noted above, in addition to your gender and race. If a search is conducted and consent is not given, you will need to make requests to the county and court of jurisdiction, as discussed later in this chapter.

Your letter might read something like this: "If there is currently a letter on file for me from my birth parents or any other relative, I would appreciate your forwarding this to me. My adopted name is Sally Smith. My date of birth is August 8, 1958. My adoptive parents are John and Sue Smith. I would like to request any identifying information you may have regarding my biological parents as provided in (refer to applicable state law here) and any identifying information you may have regarding any siblings as provided in (refer to applicable state law here). Please place this letter in any file held by your agency concerning my adoption. This letter may be used as a Waiver of Confidentiality. This includes the release of any agency records, hospital records, and court records." The state laws may be found through the Website at www.state.org.

With the information you have on hand, ask the courthouse (for the city in which your adoption took place) which court(s) handled adoptions in the year of your birth (probate, county, chancery, or circuit). Different courts may have handled adoptions, not just one, so make sure you know exactly who was responsible for court records pertaining to adoption in the years you are interested.

Once you know what court records you need to examine, understand the laws of your state regarding adoption for the year you were born. (This may be obtained through a state archives and library or law library.) You can access, by state, information about state offices, state organizations, national organizations, registries, and search or support groups by going to www.states.org on the Internet. For example, if I wanted to know how to write or call the Post Adoption Services Office in Georgia, I would first go to www.states.org/ and select Georgia. Then I would go to www.state.ga.us/ and there I would select adoption services at www.adoption.dhr.state and there I would find the information I am looking for. Some of the keywords to use on search engines include adoption offices, adoption registries, adoption laws, adoption groups, and adoption searches.

If the laws for the year you were born stated that a petition must be filed with the county court clerk's office for probate court, then this is the place to begin. Some counties may use circuit or chancery courts. Some states may have other names, so it is necessary to understand exactly what the laws were the year you were born.

Most legal adoptions require the adoptive family to file a petition requesting permission to adopt a child. This information will be recorded in a minute book, which is similar to a diary. Each minute book should also contain an index. (Entries are made daily of each case that goes before a judge, and each case is assigned a number.)

Each court keeps an account of which cases go to court in a docket appearance book, which is similar to an index. Allow for different counties to have different ways of doing this, but generally most counties will have some sort of record-keeping system similar to an index of who goes to court each day.

After all this searching, it is quite possible that you will still not have the information you need. However, if you do not attempt, you will never know.

It may be that the Waiver of Confidentiality/Request for Identifying Information will be all that is necessary. It may take a while because many others are also requesting identifying information. You may have to wait six months, but be patient; it is the best way to find out.

You may be able to obtain your information through Social Security. Others have been successful by requesting information for "humanitarian purposes." Send the information you have to:

Social Security Administration
Location Services
6401 Security Blvd.
Baltimore, MD 21235

You must enclose a letter to the person you want to contact, but do not seal the letter. It will be read to determine if it qualifies for the "humanitarian purposes" rule. Provide a name, place of birth, or any other information you know will be helpful. The letter may be forwarded to the person you are searching for if it qualifies.

Dear Norma,

My parents divorced when I was a toddler. My mother would not tell me anything about my father. She remarried and had my name changed to that of my step-father. All my life I knew this man was not my natural father. I always wanted to know about my biological father, but my mother hated him. I believe I reminded her too much of my father. She was cruel to me, both physically and mentally.

When I was about ten years old, I found a photograph of a man in an army uniform. It had a name and date on the back. At last I knew what my father looked like and what his name was—James Johnson. I kept the photograph hidden so my mother never knew. When I was twenty, I began looking for him. I traveled to many cities with my job, and the first thing I did when I arrived in a new city was to check the phone book for all the James Johnsons in that city. You can imagine how many calls (maybe thousands) I made and how much money I spent.

I have tried everything I can think of. Please help me fill the void in my life. I will not be complete until I find my father.

—JAMES

∾ ∾ ∾

Dear James,

Unfortunately, when some parents divorce they become selfish, especially when the divorce is bitter. The noncustodial parent is often left out completely. The custodial parent often wants to punish the absent parent.

Even though your mother did not tell you what you asked, the information on the back of the photograph was enough to give you hope. I'm sure you spent many nights dreaming about your father and many days wondering about him.

You may not realize it, but you have enough information to begin your search. You just don't know what to do with the information you have. Don't feel bad—most people don't know what to do with the information they have.

—NORMA

The seed for James' solution is in his letter—his parents' divorce. This is the starting point, not making random phone calls. Because he was born and raised in Nashville, Tennessee, the divorce must have taken place there because you must file for divorce in the city in which you reside (with a few exceptions). The logical place for this search to begin is the courthouse in Nashville. Once the divorce decree is examined, you should have the father's full name, date of birth, possibly a Social Security number, an employer, and a last known address. Once a person has this much information, there are several ways to locate your missing person (in this case, James' father):

- *Write for a driver's license with a name and date of birth.*
- *Write the Social Security Administration or the Internal Revenue Service and ask them to forward a letter.*

- *Run the name through an on-line phone directory (www.555-1212.com) or an e-mail directory (www.four11.com).*
- *Check the last known address for a forwarding address or neighbors who may remember the person.*
- *Check with the former employer to see if a new employer contacted that office for a reference.*
- *Check with the military records center for a military record. The Veterans' Administration might have a record of a claim for benefits. The state might have a record of an enlistment or discharge.*

Types of Adoption Searches

In response to the hundreds of adoption-related calls I have received over the years, I created the nationwide Missing Person Registry (www.reunion.com). I also began publishing the newspaper *Missing Persons*, which is circulated throughout the United States. The chances of being matched by computer or by someone seeing the search in the newspaper will greatly enhance the searcher's chances of finding the person without actually having to search physically.

One of the most important resources for an adoption searcher is to network with search and support groups. Adoption search and support groups can be found in most major cities. These groups exchange information and maintain support for their members. E-mail support lists can offer search help, support for those times when you're frustrated and ways to become active in the fight for open records. Sometimes sharing your information with a group will present a new lead that you hadn't thought of before. Those who find their missing persons often help others who are still searching. Smaller groups are usually volunteers and don't charge for their service or for membership. Large groups include the AAC-American Adoption Congress; AMFOR-Americans for Open Records; ALMA-Adoptee Liberty Movement Association; CERA-

Citizens for Equal Rights for Adoptees; CUB-Concerned United Birthparents, to name a few. Information about a few of the many e-mail support lists is available at:

> Adoptees Internet Mailing List
>> www.webreflection.com/aiml/subscribe.html
>
> Halcyon Adoption Support
>> mmci.tallynet.com/perspages/pattyann/halsearc.htm
>
> E-mail lists for specific states
>> members.tripod.com/~StateMailingLists/index.html

By the time you read this, there is no guarantee that the searchers or groups in this book will be current or that they may be able to help you. Be sure to check www.reunion.com for an updated list of adoption groups. I am listing a few samplings of the ones I have found on the Internet at this time. Use these groups or any searcher (a person you hire to do the search for you) at your own discretion. Before you pay someone to do the search for you, don't be afraid to ask for references and talk to someone who has used them. Adoption searching is the most difficult search of all and few are qualified to do it right!

A professional adoption searcher may charge an hourly rate or a flat rate. Adoption searchers may belong to a group or may be independent. It is not necessary to hire a "certified" searcher. Private investigators may work on an adoption search. However, there are only a few well-trained, experienced adoption search experts. Most private investigators will not take a case they do not intend to solve, and they should turn down or refer any work for which they are not experienced. Don't be afraid to ask for references and find out if other clients were satisfied. Licensed private investigators are governed by a board of regulators, and if they are charging for services in which they are not experienced or knowledgeable, the board may suspend their license if a complaint is received. Check with the board to see if any complaints have been lodged against a private investigator you intend to hire.

Beware of the "underground" searchers, who may get your information illegally, and for a price.

Certain states will not have open records, and finding any public source of information may be impossible. However, there are attorneys who specialize in adoption and are experienced at having court records opened. But if a searcher tells you that he or she can get you this kind of information without a court order or the legal actions of an attorney, watch out. In the states where some information is available through public records, the experienced searcher should be able to do an adoption search in a matter of weeks. It is quite possible to conduct a legal adoption search in one week. One of the secrets to conducting an adoption search is having good identifying information, such as a correct name, to begin with. Those who do not have a name will have to endure many obstacles. Keep in mind, however, that obstacles are merely opportunities in disguise. Based on my knowledge and experience, I estimate that approximately 75 percent of all adoption searchers will find the person they seek if enough information is available.

The adoption search is more involved than any other search because the search itself is only part of the process of being united (or reunited, as the case may be) with a relative. Both the searcher and the missing person will need to be prepared for the meeting. *The approach to the missing person is extremely delicate.* An inexperienced searcher could ruin a person's life if she does not understand the importance of approach and preparation. Adoption searches can be very successful, and happy outcomes are possible as long as there is a good understanding of the adoption process. Adoption search and support groups exist in every state (see Chapter Fifteen for a list). Check your telephone book for these groups, which can serve to encourage and guide you in your search.

Your individual situation will dictate which search techniques work best. And don't forget the paper trail. Besides the sources described in Chapter Five, remember these pieces of paper that might help you: hospital birth records, original birth certificate, adoption petition, adoption final decree, amended birth certificate, nonidentifying information, court order, medical records, sealed adoption records. In addition, here are several sources that many people have found useful in their adoption searches.

> *One out of every fifty people in the United States is adopted.*

Adoption Agencies

Recently, some states have passed laws requesting adoption agencies to conduct searches on behalf of adoptees and birth parents. Agencies may charge a fee for this service. If you're considering letting an agency conduct your search, make sure you understand what they can and cannot do, and what their limitations are. Don't expect more than they can give you. They are bound by law to do only what the law allows.

Both private and public adoption agencies maintain adoption records of the children they have placed. There may be as many as four copies of these sealed adoption records, with the court, the attorney, the agency, and the state. The agency should have the name, age, and general background information about the person you're looking for.

Agencies are not experienced at finding missing persons, but they may have the last known address or other vital information that will help you. Many times an agency search consists of nothing more than writing a letter to the address where the person was living when the adoption was finalized. Keep in mind that this address is as old as the adoptee. If the letter is returned as undeliverable, in most cases the search is over as far as the agency is concerned. Many of the agencies that have begun doing searches are backlogged with requests, so they may not be able to spend a lot of time on any one search.

Adoptees and/or adoptive parents who are considering having an agency do a search should be aware of one more thing. If a birth parent is located and does not react in a highly positive manner, some social workers might interpret that response as negative, and you will probably be told that the birth parent does not want any contact. (If you make contact with your missing person—in any kind of situation, not just adoption—and that person seems hesitant to speak with you, do not force the issue. Simply leave your contact information, including Social Security number in case you move. Your missing person may want to meet you later. People can change their minds when you least expect it.)

If you do not know the name of the adoption agency that handled your case, write the state Department of Human Services. Include any relevant information about your adoption, and enclose a copy of your amended birth certificate.

Classified Advertisements

If you feel certain that you're searching in the correct geographical area, try running a classified ad in the personals. When placing an ad in a public newspaper that is read by the local residents, keep in mind that identifying someone by name could be embarrassing. Here are some examples that have worked in the past:

"Looking for lost relative. Urgent medical condition. If you have any information about [Insert name] family, please contact immediately."

"Female born on January 31, 1951, urgently seeks any information regarding parents. Please call [insert telephone number]."

"REWARD: Genealogist searching for Moore family members, especially with the first name of John who lived in Tennessee between 1935 & 1950. Anyone with information, please call collect [insert telephone number]."

Other Sources

The person you are searching for might have belonged to a trade or labor union. Try requesting information contained in these records.

Professional organizations and state licensing offices are another good place to look. The National Trade and Professional Associations, published by Columbia Books, is a reference guide to more than six thousand of these organizations. Most libraries, especially those in universities and technical schools, have this book. Once you have identified an occupation (through city directories, friends, neighbors, etc.), contact the appropriate organizations.

If the doctor and/or attorneys involved in your adoption have moved, the state licensing board should be able to give you some clues to their whereabouts. Often, doctors' records are destroyed if they are deceased. However, frequently hospital records are microfilmed and stored. You may want to check the law of the state to see if you are entitled to all medical records pertaining to you. If so, that means you are entitled to your birth records.

Numerous states have a birth index in their state archives, which lists every baby born in the state. Also try looking on microfilm at a state archives and library for old adoption records from every court in the state.

If you don't find what you need here, go to a search engine and look for more. I assure you there are thousands of sites to look at. The World Wide Web has exploded with Websites authored by adoptees, birth mothers, and adoptive families. Each tells a unique story from a personal perspective. Some will even give hints they learned on their road to reunion. For example, learning to read upside down and backwards for those moments when you're speaking with someone and they have information about you right in front of them and tell you that you can't have any of it, or memorizing the adoption laws in your state for the time of your adoption and the present year-you may have to quote the law in order to get what you're after.

10

Brothers, Sisters, and Long-Lost Cousins

Finding a sibling requires the same basic information as any other search—a name for which to look. To obtain a name, you'll have to do some groundwork. Start with the information you have. How do you know there is a sibling? Who told you? Is the sibling older or younger than you? Do you know his or her birthday or place of birth?

Begin with a checklist of known information. Once you have the correct full name and date of birth, you can obtain a copy of the birth certificate from the state Office of Vital Statistics. Is your mother, father, or another relative willing to cooperate with you in your efforts?

Depending on the type of search and whether you and your sibling were separated because of adoption or nonadoption circumstances, you may already have the seed for your solution.

Dear Norma,

I am the fourth of six children. Apparently we each had different fathers. Our mother was a prostitute who entertained men in our home.

When I was eight years old, my mother had a boyfriend who told her she had to make a choice—

119

him or the three younger children. (The others had grown up and moved out.) My mother told me and my brother and sister to get in the back of her boyfriend's pickup truck. They drove us to the country, near our oldest brother's home, where we were told to get out. They drove off without saying goodbye, and my mother did not look back.

We walked to our brother's house. He was married and had a young child with a heart condition. My brother, who did not expect us that night, had a lot of medical expenses to pay. But he took us in and said he would try to raise us. We stayed with him for a few months, but times were tough and my brother could not afford to pay for us. He cried when he told us he would need to call a social worker to take us.

My two younger siblings and I were taken to a home for placement with foster families. It was like an institution. Because of the rejection, abuse, and neglect, I was angry and frustrated. I became rebellious because I felt so unloved and unwanted. I was only a small child, but it seemed no one wanted me. I thought something was wrong with me. I thought I was a bad person. I was classified as a juvenile delinquent and sent to another institution. I never saw my two younger siblings again. That was forty years ago.

Eventually I ran away and enlisted in the military. The discipline was good for me. Even though I became a responsible adult, I could not trust women, and therefore did not enjoy a relationship with a member of the opposite sex. I guess you could say that my mother had ruined my life. As I look back, I realize I was a victim.

When I was eighteen, I decided to look for my mother. I found her, married to the boyfriend. I spent a lot of time and money tracking her down. I knocked on her door and her husband answered. "What do you want?" he demanded. I told him I wanted to see my mother. I was not invited in. He called my mother to the door. "What do you want?" she asked. There was no remorse, no sign of caring, not even a friendly smile. "I just wanted to see the woman who left me on the side of the road and drove off when I was eight years old."

I walked away and never looked back. She did not attempt to stop me, or ask how my life had been, or even ask me to come in and visit. I finally accepted the fact that my mother did not want me. Until then, I think I had been in denial, trying to make excuses for her behavior.

After several years, I met a wonderful woman who understood what I had been through and why I was the way I was. She was the first person I felt loved me unconditionally. I married her and it was the best thing that ever happened to me.

I have continued to look for my two younger siblings, but I could not find them. My wife contacted the home where we were first placed and, by coincidence, my younger brother's wife had contacted them the week before. As a result, my younger brother and I have been reunited, but we cannot find our sister. We want her to know we love her and miss her.

After a lifetime of pain, anger, and hurt, finding my brother was almost a "healing" for me. I know that in order for me to heal completely I need to find my sister, too.

—RICK

≈ ≈ ≈

Dear Rick,

You are fortunate to have a wife who understood your needs and helped you find your brother. I know that you and your brother have done everything you can to locate your sister.

When I am looking for someone, I analyze what has already been done and look for what was not done. In your case, it appears you overlooked one important thing: the foster family that raised your sister may have her Social Security number.

I contacted the foster mother and explained why it was important to find your sister's Social Security number. The foster mother said she had not heard from your sister in years, but she located the information I needed. Once I had the Social Security number, I entered it into my computer and uncovered a new last name. Apparently your sister is married, with her last known address being in Florida.

With that information, I located the neighbors. I did not find a listed phone number, so I could not contact the house directly. The neighbors did not know your sister, but agreed to deliver a message to the house. A short time later, I received a call from a man who said he was divorced from your sister. He thought she was living and working in Georgia, and he provided me with an address.

I attempted to contact your sister in Georgia, but she had moved. Neighbors told me where she had worked, but the former employer did not have any information for me. It appeared that the trail had ended. (I even contacted a private investigator in Georgia and asked her to see if she could pick up a trail, but she was unable to do so.)

Several months later, I was invited to give a seminar in Georgia and decided to drive out to your sister's last known address. It was an apartment complex, and no manager was present. Your sister's apartment was empty, as was the one next door. The only

people available did not speak English. I left my
card in the door of the apartment manager. Several
days later she called to say she was new at the job,
and that she did not have a record of your sister
having lived there. And the post office did not
show a forwarding address. The trail ended once
more.

For now, I'll have to put your case aside. But trust
that I never fully quit looking for anyone, I just don't
actively pursue a search until I have a new clue.
—NORMA

*After several months, it is a good idea to review what had been done
and try again. Never, never give up! I decided to try running the
Social Security number one more time in hopes that an updated one
had been added. Sure enough, this time the sister's number had a
new address in another state.*

*I found the sister, who was in total disbelief that after all this
time her brothers finally had found her. She had lived in many states
and thought that it would be impossible for anyone to locate her. She
had given up all hope of ever finding her brothers. Knowing her
brothers cared about her was the first good thing that had happened
to her in a long time. The reason she was so hard to find? She had
been in jail.*

Siblings Looking for Siblings

Dear Norma,

I have a younger sister, Jennifer, who was adopted
as a baby. I'm sure she does not know about me. I
have wanted to find her since I was very young, but of
course I did not know where to look or how to go
about doing anything. My life will never be complete
until I find her.

Many years ago, I began asking a lot of questions
and finally traced my sister to a small town in Illinois.

I found adoption records that told me where the adoptive family had lived, but they were no longer there. I was able to find a neighbor who told me that my sister became a hairdresser and had married. She provided me the name of her husband. I thought I could locate her with that much information. I found the location of the beauty salon where she was formerly employed. However, the salon was no longer in business and I could not find anyone else who could help me. I could not find her name or the name of her husband on any records.

I don't want to give up until I find her. I have gotten so close, but it seems all the doors have suddenly closed and I don't know what else to do. Can you help?

—CHRIS

∼ ∼ ∼

Dear Chris,

You did a great search and came very close to finding your sister. With as much information as you provided me, it only took me a few hours to locate Jennifer and make contact with her. I found a new address for her in another city by accessing her forwarding address from her last known address. With the new address I was able to find new neighbors, and when I contacted the next-door neighbor, I was given the name of your sister's current employer. I contacted the employer and was told that she would be given a message to call me.

Jennifer called me as soon as she got a break. She was thrilled to know about her older sister. She knew she was adopted and had been searching for her biological mother, but did not have much information and had been unable to find her. Jennifer wanted to call you immediately, as soon as she learned about you. While we were talking, Jennifer began talking about her upcoming vacation. She said it would be a wonderful time for a family reunion. She was crying tears of happiness.

Helping people find their loved ones is one of the most gratifying pleasures I have experienced. I'm glad your lives are now complete and I wish you much happiness.

—NORMA

Chris and Jennifer ran up about a $1,000 phone bill before the family reunion, talking day and night in an attempt to make up for lost time. Chris later told me the family reunion was wonderful.

Dear Norma,

I am a thirty-two-year-old housewife with four children. For twenty years, I have been searching for my baby sister who was taken from my mother and placed for adoption. My mother has suffered three nervous breakdowns as a result of losing my sister. According to my mother, she never signed any papers relinquishing my sister. Apparently she was tricked by authorities.

My mother was born with bad eyesight, and by the time she was in the second grade she was having so much trouble that her father took her out of school and began working her in his cotton fields. My grandfather abused her for many years. By age fourteen she ran off and got married to get away from her father. She became pregnant with me. My father ran off and left her. We were forced to move in with my grandfather. My father returned the next year and my mother moved back in with him. She then became pregnant with my sister, Molly. When Molly was only a few months old, my father left again. My mother was poor, uneducated, and unable to provide for us. She signed up for welfare. My grandfather called the Department of Human Services and a social worker came to take Molly, supposedly only for a short time, while my mother looked for a job and housing. My mother was told that she could take Molly on the weekends and visit with her. Every Saturday my mother would go to the courthouse, meet the social worker, and bring Molly home. Every Sunday, my mother would take Molly back. The visitation continued for six months. Then, as usual, my mother went to pick up Molly. Instead, the social worker told my mother that Molly had been adopted by a nice family. That was it. No papers signed, no court order issued. Nothing happened before a judge. The social worker had been my mother's only contact. My mother was devastated. I was only a year and a half older than Molly, so I did not know what happened.

When I was twelve, I found a box containing some papers, including Molly's birth certificate. As my mother told me her story, I learned that she had been hospitalized with a nervous breakdown. I knew my mother was sick, but I did not know why until that time. At the age of twelve, I began looking for Molly. I even went to the courthouse in the town where we lived. I asked everyone at the courthouse to help me find my sister, but no one would help. I even located the social worker and asked her what happened to Molly, but she said she did not remember her. As I grew older, I did everything I could think of to find Molly, but no one ever helped. I wrote the state Department of Human Services, and I told them if Molly ever asked, to please give her a letter. My mother did the same.

I do not know what else to try. I have done everything I can think of. After twenty years of searching, I
have spent approximately $20,000 trying to find my
sister. I do not have any more money to spend.

Please help me find Molly.

—CAITLIN

≈ ≈ ≈

Dear Caitlin,

I have done extensive research on adoption and
am very sorry to say the adoption laws are unfair.
Unfortunately, the laws were written many years ago
and the primary purpose of the laws was to protect
the birth mother from being identified. Adoptive
families were not counseled and did not realize that
adoptees need to know their identities. Therefore, a
lot of people have suffered needlessly, especially
adoptees.

—NORMA

*The problem began when Molly was three months old, so that
served as a date to start with. Were any papers filed giving the state
authority to take Molly? Was the state appointed as guardian ad
litem for Molly? Who was legally responsible for her? The trail had to
begin at the local courthouse.*

*If Molly was adopted, the adoptive family must have filed a peti-
tion to adopt in a court, before a judge. Every courtroom keeps a
daily log of who appears, why they appeared, what the court costs
are, and so forth. This is sometimes called a docket appearance
book. The court also must keep records of what happened with each
case, recorded in minute books.*

*To find Molly, I had to look in docket appearance books and
minute books. I had to look for all the families who adopted children
the year Molly was taken from her mother. I was looking for a record
involving a three-month-old baby girl. There was only one record*

that matched. This baby was probably Molly. Her name had been changed to Angela. I copied the name of the family and found them listed in the phone book. I called the adoptive family and asked for Angela. Her adoptive mother gave me her married name. When I called Molly (Angela), I was surprised to find out that she had been searching for her biological mother for several years. She had written the state, but the state did not give her the letters written by her mother and sister. She had also been to the same courthouse that her sister and mother had visited in hopes that someone might help her.

Caitlin and Molly (Angela) had a wonderful reunion at Caitlin's home and have become the best of friends. Both of them always wished for a sister, and now they have each other.

In Search of Adopted Siblings

If your search is for an adopted brother or sister, what information do you have? Do you know the date and place of birth? Do you know the hospital? Do you know the city, county, and state of the adoption? Do you know the adoption agency that placed the child?

If you are one of the lucky ones who know the placing agency, and if it is a private rather than a public adoption agency, you are ahead of the game.

When dealing with a private agency, you may be more likely to find someone who is sympathetic to your cause, such as a social worker. Better yet, the original caseworker may be retired, which means she may feel more free to talk. The social worker who placed your sibling through a private agency may still remember the child and the family that received the child. Furthermore, the agency will probably have a record of the adoption.

Because they deal with such large numbers of babies, and have numerous social workers, public adoption agencies will most likely be less sympathetic to your efforts. (A public adoption agency places several hundred children for every one child placed by a private agency.)

If you know your birth mother, she may be willing to obtain the hospital records of your sibling's birth. The information in the medical records may identify the person who signed the baby out of the hospital, probably the social worker who delivered him or her to the adoptive or foster family. If a foster family was used before placing the baby with an adoptive family, there may be still another trail. (Courts approve and pay foster parents, so records exist.)

Some adoptions are legal and some are illegal, just as some are public and others are private. To identify the adoptive family, a search of the courthouse records of all persons who adopted a child a year or two years after the child's date of birth may turn up names of adoptive families who went through that particular court. Did other local courts also process adoptions in the years of your search? Remember that older children are adopted as well as infants, so you may want to expand the time frame of your search.

Understanding the adoption process is the key to understanding how to find a person who is adopted. (See Chapter Four and Chapter Fourteen for additional information.)

Once the adoptive family is identified, the approach must be planned and executed in such a way as to avoid hurting anyone. Although uniting siblings is not as emotionally risky as reuniting parents with their children, it still requires care and preparation. Consider having a third party make the original approach on your behalf.

If Your Sibling Was Not Adopted

It is not unusual for siblings to be separated because of divorce, and it is fairly easy to find these brothers and sisters. I like to begin with a copy of the divorce decree and obtain information on the custodial parents. It may not be necessary to get your hands on this particular decree if you have a correct name and date of birth. If you know his or her Social Security number, you are almost assured of finding your sibling.

If you are in touch with one of your birth parents, that parent can probably provide additional information, such as the names and addresses of other relatives of the former spouse. The divorced parent probably knows a lot about the person to whom he or she was married. Documents that would include a Social Security number include joint income tax returns, joint bank account statements, insurance policies, and deeds to property.

Once you've located the divorced parent, you may have the seed for solving your search. The former spouse, when found, may know where the sibling is. Finding a half-sibling involves much the same process.

If your sibling is missing because he or she left home and did not return as an adult, your search may not be all that difficult. You have to start with the same four seeds I mentioned earlier: name, date of birth, Social Security number, and last known address. Unless your brother or sister has become a voluntary missing person for some legal or financial reason, is a criminal, or is under protection by the government, or is out of the country, those four pieces of information can take you a long way toward your missing sibling.

If you are searching for a lost brother or sister, you certainly aren't alone. I receive hundreds of letters each year detailing the anguish of separated siblings.

Congratulations! You've Just Inherited . . .

The primary difference between heir or beneficiary searching and a normal search for a missing sibling is that you have little information to go on. Usually a name is all there is. In that case, it is up to the searcher to take that name, whether it is common or uncommon, and make the most of it.

The seed for finding the missing person may be contained in the obituary of the deceased. By studying every piece of information available about the deceased, it is possible to determine the next of kin at the time of death and to get a copy of the death certificate, as well as funeral and cemetery records. (Don't overlook Social Security, census records, insurance, or veterans' benefits that may have paid funeral expenses.)

Back to the Basics

Once you've gleaned everything you can about the person in question, you'll need to begin with a plan, and write everything down. Who are you searching for? What do you know about that person? Who can provide additional information?

Obtain as much information as possible from relatives, family Bibles, birth certificates, death certificates, obituaries, and other documents.

Write down everything you learn about the missing person in chronological order. As you learn more, add it to your list, which hopefully will include by this time: correct, full name; date and place of birth; and last known address.

Explore sources of additional information through various reference resources. For example: Internet—white pages (www.whowhere.com/phone.html), yellow pages (www.lookupusa.com/), e-mail directories (www.infop.com), and reverse white pages (www.isleuth.com); state archives and library—old directories; war records; census records; birth records; courthouse—probate records; property records; marriage/divorce documentation; state offices—birth and death records; federal offices—Social Security; military; Veterans' Administration; and Bureau of the Census.

Have a checklist of things to do and places to go. For example: "Call or write for a document, certificate, or other record."; "Go to archives library and look at a 1920 Census microfilm."; "Check public library for obituary in old newspaper."; or "Contact information broker."

11

Best Friends and
First Loves

WHY DO BEST friends and first loves go their separate ways? There may have been a quarrel, a departure for college, a death, a divorce, a broken heart, a bad decision, or an unplanned journey. Whatever the reason for the separation, the time may eventually come when one or the other longs for a reunion.

To find someone you have not seen for many years, you will have to begin with whatever information you have available. As with any search, this one will be easier if you have a name, a date of birth, last known address, or a Social Security number.

Dear Norma,

I am searching for a lost loved one. I met this man in New Hampshire the summer of 1957. I fell deeply in love with him but lost contact when my aunt and uncle, with whom I was staying, moved from Rye, New Hampshire, to Merideth, New Hampshire. I married and divorced, but never stopped loving this man.

I would like to know if he's married and happy, or even still alive. I want to be able to rest my heart and dreams of knowing one way or another.

I'm sure you've been bombarded with a lot of requests. My family thinks I'm odd and am batting zero here. Maybe I am. Maybe he wouldn't even remember me, but I would like to find out. Thanks in advance for your help.

Sincerely,
—SHANNON

Dear Mrs. Tillman,

I am looking for my first love. He is the father of my oldest son. He was in the Corps of Engineers. U.S. Army, stationed at Ft. Lewis, Washington, in 1941 or 1942.

My son has never seen his father. I am sixty-eight and his father was older than me. He was from Leeville, Louisiana. Please help me find this man.

Yours truly,
—ANN

               ≋ ≋ ≋

Norma,

To me, friendship is something that should last forever.

When I was a child I went to my grandmother's every summer. She lived in Nashville, Tennessee. I met Sandy and we would stay together the whole summer. When I became a teenager, I still went to Tennessee and Sandy and I would trade clothes, go to the stock car races, and go out on dates with boys. Then we both graduated from high school. Sandy invited me to her wedding and I caught her flowers. I married and she and I saw each other once in a while.

She divorced and married several more times, and we just lost contact. I have found out that she married again and is living somewhere either in North or South Carolina. I have been married to the same man for twenty-nine years.

Maybe if I could find out what her name is now I could find out where Sandy is. Could you tell me how I could find that information?

Oh, by the way, I have two grown boys and am the grandmother of two beautiful grandchildren. So you see, Sandy and I have a lot of catching up to do!

Thank you so much.

—VICKI

Ask Yourself Some Questions

In addition to knowing your missing person's name, there are some other issues to consider:

How did you know this person?
Where did he live?
Where did she work?
Where did she attend school?
Who were your mutual friends?
What do you know about the family?
Is the last name unusual or common?
What was the last year you knew him?

Check the Internet phone directores (www.whowhere. com/phone.html) or e-mail directories (www.infop.com) in the city in which your friend lived. You can also go to the local library in that city (or call the reference librarian if you no longer live there) and look in the crisscross, or cross-reference, directory for the year that you were last in touch with your friend, searching for the last name of the person you seek. Obtain a list of all the individuals with that last name who appear in the directory.

Cities of fewer than fifty thousand people may not have a crisscross directory. If you are dealing with a small town, the library will have old telephone books. Use the reference material that is available. Find out if there are any library volunteers or county historians who could assist you. Almost every town has a historical society with people who enjoy researching families who lived there. There is possibly a genealogist you can call. Small towns often have family cemeteries and the town historian may know where they are located. Someone will help you if you cannot physically do the research yourself.

Who Remembers?

Use your imagination. If nothing else works, you can always place a classified ad in the local newspaper. Ask that anyone with information about this family please contact you.

Here are some other hints:

- School teachers often remember their students.
- Mail carriers remember the people on their routes.
- Church directories list members.
- Cemeteries keep records of all people buried there.
- Funeral homes have records of funerals.
- Courthouses have marriage, divorce, and other records.

Depending on what information you have on this missing person, it is possible in some states to write for a driver's license, vehicle registration, birth records (for an estimated year), and even divorce records. If you remember your friend's former employer, or the school the person attended, try finding someone at either of those places who might give you information. I find neighbors and former neighbors to be excellent sources of information.

First Loves

Your first love may have been in your life many years ago, when you were both very young. You probably have a thousand wonderful memories but precious little information. In most cases, the only thing you know about your first love is a first and last name, possibly a former address, and perhaps a school he or she attended. If it was a girlfriend, her name may have changed more than once since you knew her.

Most people who fall in love when they are very young do not care about personal information and have no need for their lovers' birth date, Social Security number, and, in some cases, even their full name. For some, the meeting may have occurred away from a hometown, during a spring break or a vacation. Often, a first love is a person you know very little about. The less you know, the harder you'll have to work to remember every detail, no matter how insignificant it seems.

Whatever information you can remember is all you'll have to work with. It helps if your first love has an unusual last name, because then you can search the entire United States by computer. If you know the city you can search the phone directories on the Internet (www.555-1212.com) or e-mail addresses (www.four11.com) the world over.

With only a surname search, it is possible to find the missing person. I have found many people by checking the death records for all persons who died between certain years with the last name of the person I sought. By finding a death record, I find out where the final Social Security payment was made (the last address of the deceased). I also have a date of death, so I am able to check a newspaper for the obituary, which usually lists survivors. By finding survivors, I find the missing person.

No matter what information you begin with, there is *almost* always a trail to follow.

If your first love was someone you went to high school or college with, check with the class representative for the school alumni association. If this does not work, try locating someone who works with school records. Checking old yearbooks and directories may provide a clue. If confidentiality rules prevent you from contacting the person directly, see if someone will relay a message for you, asking your missing person to call or write you. More often than not, someone will cooperate.

Did your first love attend church? Churches maintain records for many years. I have never been turned down for help by a church secretary. As long as you remain nonthreatening to anyone you contact for information, you should not have a problem.

Getting Nowhere Fast?

If you are unable to get information by telephoning, writing, or asking in person, something may be wrong with the way you are inquiring. Practice asking nonthreatening questions in a direct and an indirect manner.

Check your tone of voice. Take note of your mannerisms. Listen to the way you phrase your questions. Polish your charisma. Be as nice as you can be, even if the person does not help. And don't be afraid to smile.

As with any search for a missing person, the approach is important. Disrupting another person's life with an inappropriate approach can be disastrous. Once contact is made, you will be able to determine whether your "best friend" is glad to hear from you, whether your "first love" is now married, and whether you should pursue the possibility of an ongoing relationship.

Tips for Best Friend and First Love Searchers

As you look for your first love or an old friend, remember that "no" only means "maybe." Obstacles are opportunities in disguise.

Here are some tips for finding your best friend or first love:

1. Make sure you have the correct name.

2. Try to obtain his last known address.

3. If you know a birthdate for a man, try looking for a driver's license. (A man will be easier to locate because his name should not have changed as might a married woman's.)

4. Search the Internet for a phone number (www.yahoo. com/search/people) or e-mail address (www.four11.com).

5. If you know a female's father's or brother's name, try looking for him and see if he'll tell you where she is.

6. If you have a last known address, contact neighbors to see if anyone remembers the person or the family. Older neighbors are excellent contacts.

   Ask a librarian, historian, genealogist, or library volunteer to help you research records and find a former address or other information about your missing person.

7. If the person you seek was born prior to 1920, look for a census listing.

   If the person you seek was in the military, try calling or writing a regional Veterans' Administration (VA) office (information can be found in Chapter Fifteen) and ask if the person has filed a claim for any type of benefit. Make up a date of birth if you have to give one. The VA will verify if the person has filed a claim. By asking for the claim number, you will receive either a Social Security number or a service I.D. number. With a Social Security number, an information broker may be able to trace this person through various databases.

12

Men and Women in Uniform: Military Searches

THE MOST COMMON military search is for a father. However, often military friends and buddies who have lost touch over the years decide they want to find each other. Sharing the experience of military life makes service people as close as families. Some would even say that soldiers who fight together in the heat of battle become blood brothers.

If the person you are seeking is on active duty, there are military locating services for every branch of the service. If you know where the person is stationed, perhaps someone there will forward a message to the person you seek.

In one case, I called after 5:00 p.m. on a Friday, needing to speak with someone before Monday. I left a message for the chaplain to call me back, and he did so in about an hour. I asked if he could deliver a message to my missing person. The next day, my call was returned.

Dear Norma,

My parents divorced when I was six. I have two sisters. My father was a career military officer and was seldom at home. He lived in other countries and we hardly knew him. I barely remember him, but I know I loved him very much and missed him.

After the divorce, my mother remarried and I was raised by a nice stepfather, although he could never fill the shoes of my real father.

I am now thirty-three years old, married, and have three children. My mother died eight years ago. During this time, someone at the funeral home took a call from my father, who apparently had been notified of my mother's death. None of our family was there at the time and we only got a message that he called. We were told that he was calling from the Seoul Garden Hotel in Seoul, South Korea. We never heard from him again.

I have contacted the military, written Social Security, and done everything I can think of to locate my father, but I have not been successful. Can you please help me find my father?
—ROB

≈ ≈ ≈

Dear Rob,

I requested information from the Records Center in St. Louis, Missouri, to no avail. However, your problem contained the seed for the solution! Your father was at the Seoul Garden Hotel. I have a large directory of hotels around the world and I looked up the Seoul Garden. They had a fax listed. I faxed a letter to the hotel manager and explained that I was trying to help you find your father.

Sixteen days later, the hotel manager faxed me back. He knew your father personally and gave me his address and phone number. Your father was retired,

but still living in Seoul. The manager had contacted
your father and given him my letter.
—NORMA

The next day, Rob's father called me. When I told him that his chil-
dren were looking for him, he began sobbing. He said he had tried for
many years to locate his children, but because they had moved he
could not find them. He wanted to talk to his children immediately.
He told me that he would never lose contact with them again.

Dear Norma,

As an eighteen-year-old soldier in Vietnam in the
1970s, you can imagine how homesick I became. I
had never been away from home before and I was
scared to death.

When I went to boot camp, I met Jack, from my
home state of Kentucky. Jack and I became the best of
friends, but were separated with our duty assignments.
Imagine the thrill I felt when he was assigned to my
unit in Vietnam. We hadn't seen each other for a
long time, but it was like being reunited with a member of my family. We were inseparable and I cared for
him like a brother.

After we got out of the service and returned
home, we lost contact. It has been fourteen years
since I have seen Jack and I would like very much to
find him and renew our friendship. I have attempted
to find him at the address I had for him fourteen years
ago, but apparently he has moved. I moved also, so if
he tried to find me, I was not there either.

Please help me find my "brother." I really have
missed him and would like to know what he has done
since I last saw him. Most of all, I'd like for him to
meet my family.
—BOB

Dear Bob,

Sometimes the obvious can seem to be invisible. You knew your friend's full name, date of birth, and last known address. Almost anyone can be found with that much information! You just did not know what to do with what you had.

All I had to do was check for a vehicle registered to him. I found him in about ten minutes. I wish all my searches were this easy.

—NORMA

Bob and Jack have vowed not to lose touch with one another again. The last I heard from them, they were planning to spend their vacation together. I love happy endings!

Consider the Possibilities

A good place to start is the Internet. There is a National Personnel Records Center that maintains a Website (www.nara.gov/regional/mpr.html) where visitors can download and print the necessary forms to request military personnel, health, and medical records for millions of discharged and deceased veterans from all services. Unfortunately, because of the Privacy Act of 1974, the center does not offer an e-mail based request for records or an on-line database, rather it requires a written, signed, and dated request on paper. Still, the site is useful for determining what is available and how to get it.

None of the services offers an on-line Locator service. Their Websites have general information (including telephone numbers) on how to find people on active duty. Here are the official home pages and phone numbers for each service:

Army	www.army.mil	(314) 538-4261
Navy	www.navy.mil	(314) 538-4141
Air Force	www.af.mil	(314) 538-4243
Marines	www.usmc.mil	(314) 538-4141
Coast Guard	www.uscg.mil	(314) 538-4141

Many military publications exist in which you could run a classified ad. Many libraries contain service information. Each state has a list of military personnel who either enlisted or were discharged from that state. The National Archives has regional records centers around the country. There are plenty of ways to locate someone who was in the military.

Overseas searchers may be looking for an American father or friend who was stationed in a foreign country. These people may not realize that there are many sources who can help them, even if they cannot come to the United States. If someone from another country has nothing but a name, it is possible to find the name in a computer database. The Veterans of Foreign Wars, American Legion, and other organizations maintain membership lists.

If you know the name, branch of military, dates of service, places stationed, or other information about someone in the military, it is possible to find the person. It may take a lot of research, but there are various ways of locating almost anyone who is—or was—in the military. One of the most useful public databases is the Department of Defense Alumni Search Form that can be found at the US Army Home Page under Alumni Index (www.army.mil/vetinfo/default.htm). The database contains contact names and numbers for every military alumni organization.

When speed is the main objective, the best way of finding a current or former service member is through a paid commercial site. The field gets a little more crowded each year, but only two companies appear to be worth the money when it comes to military records.

The Army Times Publishing Co., which publishes the most popular and widely read newspapers for military people, offers searchable databases containing 10 million records for active-duty service members, retirees, and National Guard and Reserve Members. To gain access to the databases and unlimited searches, go to Military City On-line (www.militarycity. com) and register to become a member at either $4 a month or $36 a year. In addition to the databases, members have access to four years worth of archives for all of the military newspapers, including *Army Times*, *Navy Times*, *Air Force Times*, and the Marine Corps edition of *Navy Times*.

A more expensive and extensive collection of databases is operated by Ameridex Information Systems (kadima.com). Visitors to this Website can search through six databases including a five-million-name listing of military people and the Nationwide Death Index. The service can get expensive, though, because it charges fifty dollars just to enroll, and each search—even unsuccessful ones—is charged individually at one to three dollars per search.

Veterans

There are approximately 27 million living veterans, including 100,000 veterans of World War I, more than 9 million veterans of World War II, 5 million veterans of the Korean War, and more than 8 million veterans of the Vietnam War who are still living.

Some government agencies, such as Social Security, Internal Revenue Service, and the Veterans' Administration may have a current address for your missing military person. There may an office of disclosure within one of these agencies that, upon written request, will forward a letter to a relative.

To have a letter forwarded, you will need to prepare two separate letters. One will be sent to the office of disclosure requesting the enclosed letter be forwarded. Explain briefly your relationship to the veteran, with as much identifiable information as possible about yourself and the veteran. If possible, include some form of identification, such as a birth certificate. Enclose the second letter in an unsealed, stamped envelope with the name and service I.D. number of the veteran written on the front of the envelope. You will be notified if your veteran cannot be identified or if the post office is unable to deliver your letter. Before trying to have a letter forwarded, it is advisable to contact one of the regional offices of the VA to verify if a death benefit has been paid or a claim filed. If the VA regional office furnishes you information, include this with your letter. Make your letter simple and straightforward.

When requesting information pertaining to veterans, it is advisable to obtain the correct mailing address for the office. To contact the nearest VA regional office call (800) 827-1000 and you will be automatically connected. You may verify that a veteran is listed in their files before you mail your correspondence. The more information you can provide, the easier it will be for someone to locate your missing person. If you do not have a full name, date of birth, branch of service, the city and state where the person entered the service, and/or Social Security or service I.D. number, ask if the person you seek has filed a claim. If so, ask for the claim number, which is usually the service I.D. number or the Social Security number.

The VA has addresses—current at the time of application for or receipt of benefits—of veterans who have applied for benefits, such as educational assistance, medical care, disability, pensions, loans, insurance, and death. VA insurance offices have information that is not available to the regional offices.

Veterans' Administration
Dept. of Veterans' Affairs Insurance Service
P.O. Box 13399
Philadelphia, PA 19101
(800) 669-8477
To contact the VA office nearest you, call (800) 827-1000.

For veterans who have been separated for less than five years, contact:
OSGLI (Office of Service Group Life Insurance)
213 Washington Street
Newark, NJ 07102-2999
(800) 419-1473

To have a letter forwarded to a veteran:
Dept. of Veterans' Affairs
Veterans' Benefits Administration
Administrative Support Staff (20A52)
810 Vermont Ave., NW
Washington, DC 20420

A list of regional VA offices can be found in Chapter Fifteen.

Military Rosters

The VA National Personnel Records Center (NPRC) in St. Louis, Missouri, is responsible for researching rosters of large groups of veterans. The charge is about $2 per name to be researched, payable to Department of Veterans' Affairs. When requesting information, include the veteran's name and service number. If you do not have the service number, try to provide one or more of these pieces of identifying information: full name; date of birth; Social Security number; city and state of enlistment; and branch of service.

The records center will provide you with the following information for each name you submit: VA file or claim number; VA regional office where file is located; If death benefits were applied, the date of death; If no benefits were applied for, notification that no record exists; No information if you did not provide correct information, or they could not locate a record based on the facts you submitted.

The VA claim number, file number, service I.D. number, or Social Security number may be the same. Since June 1974, the

VA has used one's Social Security number as the VA claim number.

The National Personnel Records Center

The National Personnel Records Center (NPRC) may forward a letter to a veteran if the requestor qualifies under the following permissible purposes:

1. Requestor's VA/Social Security benefits are dependent on contacting the veteran (dependent relative).
2. Veteran's benefits will be affected.
3. The letter to be forward is in the best interest of the veteran, as in probating a will or settling an estate in which the veteran may be involved.
4. A legitimate effort to claim a debt by a financial institution.

A fee of $3.50 will be charged if the correspondence is not in the veteran's interest, such as debt collection.

If the NPRC forwards your letter to the veteran and it is not delivered, you will not be notified.

A federal court decision in 1990 directed the NPRC to forward letters to the last known address of veterans who may have fathered illegitimate children who are members of an organization called War Babes. (These children were fathered by U.S. servicemen while in Great Britain during World War II.)

In 1973, a fire at the NPRC destroyed about 80 percent of the records for army personnel discharged between November 1, 1912, and January 1, 1960. (About 75 percent of the records for air force personnel with surnames from Hubbard through Z who were discharged between September 25, 1947, and January 1, 1964, were also destroyed.)

State adjutants general and state veterans' offices keep war records, including all enlistments and discharges in that state. The state archives will also have military records. Contact:

National Personnel Records Center
9700 Page Blvd.
St. Louis, MO 63132

Military Organizations

Most military, veterans', and patriotic organizations have newsletters and magazines that provide news about forthcoming reunions. They run lists of veterans who are being sought to notify them of the reunions. When requesting military information always be prepared to provide as much identifying information as possible, such as full name, date of birth, Social Security number, or service I.D. number. Usually military organizations do not charge a fee for locator services, such as forwarding a letter to present or former members.

These Websites are generally less accurate than using paid databases. But for people with more specialized searches, they should fit the bill.

Military USA (www.militaryusa.com) offers a free, 2.7 million-name database of Vietnam Veterans and links to several other services—including the fee-based service operated by Ameridex.

Sailors Lost and Found (www.hislight.com/sailors) offers a self-reported registry of people who served in the Navy, although its accuracy is questionable since all the information is unverified. There is a similar Website called Semper Fi (coyote.csusm.edu/public/netnav/semper_fi/lost.htm) dedicated to Marines. For finding children of military people, the Military Brats Registry (www.military-brats.com) is the best source on the Web.

Although the World Wide Web is the hottest place on the Internet, there are several other places in cyberspace that could be helpful. To post a message to an electronic bulletin board, try Military City Online on the America Online service (keyword MCO). Operated by Army Times Publishing Co., this site contains hundreds of messages posted by current and former military people—many of whom are willing to aid in a search. But be forewarned: posting a message on a bulletin board is a little like yelling, "Where's Mike?" at a crowded party.

On the Internet, bulletin boards are known as newsgroups. To post to one, etiquette dictates that you join the newsgroup (it's free) and read some postings before asking any of your own questions. In other words, you have to be patient. Some of the more useful newsgroups include alt.military.retired, soc.veteran, us.military.army, and alt.culture.military-brats.

Tips for Military Searches

1. Write the National Personnel Records Center for Information. A request form is available in this book and at the Office of Regional Records Services Website (www.nara.gov/regional/mpr.html).

2. Check the following Websites for information:

Military Airplane Accident Reports:
www.member.aol.com
e-mail: accreport@aol.com
Military Searches and Reunions:
www.reunion.com
Korean War Project:
www.onramp.net
Remembrance (Vietnam):
www.vietvet.org
Virginia Military Institute Archives:
www.vmi.edu
Library of Congress:
lcweb2.loc.gov
American Civil War Links:
www.geocities.com

Civil War Ancestors:
www.itd.nps.gov
The Civil War Trust:
www.civilwar.org
The American Civil War Archives:
www.access.digex.net
Civil War General Interest Links:
fly.hiwaay.net
Civil War: Resources on the Internet:
www.dsu.edu
Ultimate Civil War Reference Manual:
www.erols.com

3. An information broker can possibly find this person with a name only (see Chapter Fifteen for a list of information brokers).

4. If the person you are looking for died in service, write The National Cemetery System (810 Vermont Avenue. Northwest, Washington, DC 20420) with your request. Be sure to include all identifying information. They have records for almost all military people who are buried in national cemeteries in the United States.

13

The Buck Stops Here: Deadbeat Dads and Other People Who Owe Money

THE MAJORITY OF parents who don't pay child support are fathers, but it is understood that both fathers and mothers may owe back child support. I will refer to the father as the person who owes child support to keep this simple, but that isn't always the case.

Most fathers are not hardened criminals, and they feel they got a bad deal. They either cannot or will not pay their obligations. They disappear to avoid legal complications.

Of course, absent fathers are not the only kinds of people who owe money. All sorts of people who have debts to pay may try their hand at disappearing.

Dear Norma,

My husband owes me more than $18,000 in back child support. I have a court order for his arrest if he can be located. I'm sure he has a good job and can afford to pay this, but he has chosen to deny his responsibility. I have had to struggle to support our children.

I have waited for the local child-support collection office to find him for five years, but nothing has happened. It seems like they are not even trying to find him or do anything. In our state, once a father fails to pay back child support, he is subject to arrest until the debt is paid.

Sincerely,

—BARBARA

～ ～ ～

Dear Barbara,

Although the numbers will vary according to population, if you use your city of approximately 500,000 people as an example, there could be as many as 50,000 other mothers in your city experiencing the same problem.

With the information you furnished, I was able to locate your former husband in two days. I even found where he was employed and delivered a copy of the warrant for his arrest to the local sheriff's office. Your former husband was picked up and taken to jail from his office. Within three hours, his parents had paid all back child support and bailed him out of jail.

Sincerely,

—NORMA

This man could have paid what he owed, but he chose not to. He had almost all of his assets, including his home, bank accounts, vehicles, and other property in his parents' names. He tried to hide so no one could force him to pay, but it did not work. If he had not had the assets, or his family had not helped him, he would have remained in jail indefinitely until the debt was paid.

The typical missing father probably has moved to another state hoping he is safe. There are many Websites you can access on the Internet when looking for a deadbeat parent. A good one is the Federal Office of Child Support Enforcement (www.acf.dhhs.gov/ACFPrograms/CSE/index.html). This Website contains information—from all fifty states—on how to collect child support. All you do is click on the state that you want and it automatically connects you.

The Child Support Enforcement (CSE) Program is a federal/state/local effort to locate parents, their employers, and/or their assets; establish paternity if necessary; and establish and enforce child support orders. State and local CSE offices provide day-to-day operation of the program. When a parent has disappeared, it is usually possible for the CSE office to find him/her with the help of other state agencies, such as the Department of Motor Vehicles, or the Federal Parent Locator Service. He may try not to leave a paper trail but will continue to live a normal lifestyle. He may own a home, a car, be employed, attend church, have credit cards, be a member of a club or organization, have friends, and visit or contact relatives. How does he pay rent? Utilities? Does he live with someone? Is he self-employed, employed, disabled, or unemployed?

This type of missing person will maintain contact with someone. He is cautious about returning for fear a warrant will be served on him. He feels safe as long as he is far away. There is a chance (however slight) that he will change his identity. He will most likely have an unlisted telephone, use a post office box for mail, and have his property in someone else's name, but he will probably still use his correct date of birth and Social Security number. On the chance that his/her phone number is listed, there are search engines on the Web to help locate deadbeat parents. Four11 (www.four11.com) is the Website for telephone results by the yahoo search engine. It will search by name for a listed phone number in the state you select. The search engine Database America (www.databaseamerica.com) will search the selected state by phone number or by name. These databases are self-explanatory and easy to use.

He may even remarry and have a new family. Whatever interests and hobbies he once enjoyed, he will continue to enjoy. This missing person will not expect to be caught and will be completely off guard if you do not ask too many questions or talk to anyone who might tip him off. This type of person will run the minute he thinks someone is looking for him. Extreme caution must be taken so that the missing person is unaware someone is looking for him. This can be done in various ways.

One method is to have someone get close to his best friend or closest relative and be very nonthreatening. Without asking direct questions, it is possible to learn much information. Asking the right questions takes a lot of planning and skill. It is possible to talk to someone about something totally unrelated and casually mention something that will make the person you are talking to volunteer the information you are really after.

Until you are proficient in this technique, I do not recommend that you use it. Develop the skill with practice and experience. Talk to people you know. See how much information they will tell you without your asking directly for it. Learn to push the buttons of the person you are talking to. Learn to ask indirect questions that will result in the answers you actually seek.

The parent who has skipped out without paying child support will probably have a driver's license with his correct name and date of birth on it. You should always take a look at the missing person's driving history. Perhaps there has been a traffic violation or an accident. This information could divulge the person's whereabouts. The vehicle that was driven before the disappearance could be the same vehicle being driven now. While it may have a new license plate, the vehicle identification number will remain the same no matter where the missing person goes. By obtaining a copy of the missing person's vehicle title and registration you can also obtain the vehicle's identifi-

> *When Dad runs away, Mom loses money, but the*
> *kids lose their father.*

cation number. This number can be traced to a new license number and a new address. It may be possible to obtain this information with only a name.

Not every state will accommodate searchers, but the majority will. You may write one letter and have it photocopied fifty times, then mail each state a request for a search for that vehicle identification number. Each state that offers this service will charge a small fee, usually less than $10.

There are a number of government agencies that work on finding deadbeat parents to collect back child support and prosecute these evaders. However, the number of deadbeats far outnumbers the government's resources in this field. You can e-mail the White House (www.whitehouse.gov) to make sure the government is doing everything in its power to find these deadbeats. If the government seems to be getting nowhere, there are outside child support collection agencies, such as Support Kids (www.supportkids.com), that can help you collect the money you deserve.

Another way to locate people using the Web is through newsgroups. You leave messages for people and if they want, they can answer you by sending a message themselves to the board. You have the opportunity to put into words the thoughts and facts that have been floating around your head. This helps you to realize what you know, what you need to know, and how irritating the search has already been. People reading these messages have been in similar situations and understand the difficulties of searching for deadbeats. Someone may even offer advice as to how to avoid future complications. This is one of the more chancy ways to obtain information, but I have left messages on the boards and have had government agencies from other states contact me so I know it can work. There are two message boards that I have found to be very helpful: alt child support and Missing Persons Cybercenter (hollywoodnetwork.com/hn/mpc/mailroom/board.html#1463). These and other newsgroups can be found by searching the Deja News search engine (www.dejanews.com). Newsgroups are a good place to solicit advice and help you keep your sanity by offering a place to vent your frustration when faced with dead ends.

Some people who owe money never intended to have a financial problem. Thus they were emotionally unprepared when it hit; they panicked and saw no way out except to run. This is often the case with a deadbeat dad. He may be in debt to begin with. When the court orders him to pay child support, he may have to take on an extra job. If he still cannot come up with the money, he risks going to jail.

Whatever his reason for not paying, he probably won't be able to see his child because of the financial default. Children are always the victims of divorce. And when money comes between them and their fathers, they lose again. Not only have they lost a two-parent home, now they've lost the security, stability, love, and nurture that their father can provide, even if they do not see him on a daily basis.

Dear Norma,

I represent a client who owns a carpet business. My client extended credit of more than $10,000 to a man named Ken Roberts, who remodeled homes. Mr. Roberts gave false information on his credit application and my client failed to verify the information.

Mr. Roberts has disappeared. Efforts to contact him at the address furnished on his application proved to be unsuccessful as the address was a vacant lot. The phone number was a pay phone booth. Nothing on his application was true, except his name.

With only a name to work with, is it possible to locate Mr. Roberts?

Sincerely,

—K. JONES, ATTORNEY

≈ ≈ ≈

Dear Mr. Jones,

It seems that for every pound of lies therein lies at least an ounce of truth. Such is the case with K. Roberts. He used his correct name.

Because your client has a judgment against Mr. Roberts, and I am actually being paid directly by your client, and because Mr. Roberts signed a release for checking his credit, I obtained a copy of Mr. Roberts' credit report.

From Mr. Roberts' credit report, I learned that a recent inquiry was made from a car dealer near Atlanta, Georgia. I contacted the car dealer and located a salesman who recently sold him a vehicle. The salesman was kind enough to check his records to identify Mr. Roberts' employer.

With this information, I contacted the employer and verified employment, so you can garnishee Mr. Roberts' wages.

Sincerely,

—NORMA

Because Roberts is a fairly common name, I chanced that I could find him in my computer with a surname search. Thus I was able to find his new address in Alpharetta, Georgia, and Mr. Jones was able to collect his judgment.

A Breed unto Themselves

Deadbeat dads and skiptracers are missing persons who are deliberately hiding because they owe money. They usually leave a

> **Missing persons take their habits and hobbies with them. These activities may provide clues.**

trail, or at least a few good clues, because they are not professional criminals, although some of them may be borderline crooks.

Individuals like this continue to survive despite the fact that they owe money. To do so, they require an income. Identifying this source of revenue may be almost impossible, especially if they are self-employed, which is common with this particular group. They may have a business license accessible only by the name of the business.

The person who owes money will try to hide to avoid being found and made to pay. This sort of missing person probably fears that every time he answers the phone or opens the door it will be a bill collector, a process server, or even the Internal Revenue Service.

Leaving a Paper Trail

The person who disappears owing money is a voluntary missing person. Not being a professional criminal, this type of person does not know how to avoid leaving a paper trail. The missing person simply moves away and tries to start over. Nevertheless, he is probably going to become lax after a while. Once he gets comfortable in his new life, he begins to leave a new trail. As long as no one has bothered him, he eventually begins to feel secure.

Voluntary missing persons work, own a car, buy a home, and act like everyone else. There is nothing different about these people, other than the fact that they owe someone money and cannot or will not pay it back. Finding their paper trail begins with clues from information known about them before they disappeared. For them to live normally, they have to have certain necessities, which may include: driver's license; vehicle registration; voter's registration; taxes assessed on property owned; financial records; contact with relatives and friends; recreational activities and hobbies; clubs, groups, organizations, and religious institutions.

Whatever the reason for their departure, missing people who owe money have to eat, find shelter, and be transported from one place to another. Unless they've changed their Social Security number and/or date of birth (which involves some fairly risky dealings) or failed to use it, they are trackable.

Tips for Finding People Who Owe Money

1. Learn the full correct name of your target person.

2. Get the date of birth (for discovering driving history).

3. Find out if the person you're searching for is dead, look up the Social Security Death Index (www.ancestry.com/ssdi).

4. Obtain a Social Security number (and hope it is correct!). That number is a universal tracking number and one of the keys to various databases. Maybe your target will use it for credit purposes in another state.

5. Did he own a vehicle? If so, obtain the title and registration. The vehicle identification number remains with the vehicle and is a good tracking number. Your insurance agent possibly can check an insurance database to see if the missing person has any kind of insurance. If an agent can help you, look for medical claims, automobile insurance, and life insurance.

6. A former girlfriend or spouse who is angry at the target will be an excellent source of information. His enemies are your best friends!

7. Unsuspecting relatives may know of the debtor's whereabouts but probably will not cooperate. It is up to you to find a friendly, nonthreatening way to make contact with a relative or friend. The indirect approach is best.

8. Neighbors and former business associates may provide new clues.

9. Other persons may also be looking for him for collection purposes. Maybe by pooling your resources and sharing and comparing information, everyone involved will have a better chance of locating the person and claiming their money.

State Child Support Enforcement offices

Alabama	(205) 242-9300	Montana	(406) 442-7278
Alaska	(907) 276-3441	Nebraska	(402) 471-9160
Arizona	(602) 252-0236	Nevada	(702) 687-4744
Arkansas	(501) 682-8398	New Hampshire	(603) 271-4426
California	(916) 654-1556	New Jersey	(609) 588-2361
Colorado	(303) 866-5994	New Mexico	(505) 827-7200
Connecticut	(203) 566-3053	New York	(518) 474-9081
Delaware	(302) 577-4863	North Carolina	(919) 571-4120
DC	(202) 724-8800	North Dakota	(701) 224-3582
Florida	(904) 488-9900	Ohio	(614) 752-6561
Georgia	(404) 657-3851	Oklahoma	(405) 424-5871
Guam	(671) 475-3360	Oregon	(503) 986-2417
Hawaii	(808) 587-3700	Pennsylvania	(717) 787-3672
Idaho	(208) 334-5710	Puerto Rico	(809) 722-4731
Illinois	(217) 782-8768	Rhode Island	(401) 277-4731
Indiana	(317) 233-5437	South Carolina	(803) 737-5870
Iowa	(515) 281-5580	South Dakota	(605) 773-3641
Kansas	(913) 296-3237	Tennessee	(615) 741-1820
Kentucky	(502) 564-2285	Texas	(512) 463-2181
Louisiana	(504) 342-4780	Utah	(801) 536-8500
Maine	(207) 287-2886	Vermont	(800) 786-3214
Maryland	(410) 333-3979	Virginia	(804) 692-1428
Massachusetts	(617) 727-4200	Washington	(360) 586-3162
Michigan	(517) 373-7570	West Virginia	(304) 558-3780
Minnesota	(612) 296-2542	Wisconsin	(608) 266-9909
Mississippi	(601) 359-4500	Wyoming	(307) 777-6948
Missouri	(314) 751-4301		

14

Tracing Your Family Tree

TRACING YOUR family tree can be as much fun as a treasure hunt. You never know where you might have to look to find your treasure: information about your family.

When you begin to trace your family tree, it is important to realize the value of every piece of information, no matter how insignificant it may seem. Each piece will lead to another piece. Every single name, address, date of birth, place of birth, place of death, and all survivors must be carefully examined and analyzed.

> *Dear Norma,*
>
> After watching you on the "Sally Jessy Raphael" show, I thought you could help me. I am in the process of tracing my family tree and would appreciate any help or advice that you could offer. I have already traced my mother's family history back to our Jewish ancestors in Europe, but I would like to continue my search.
>
> Please contact me if you can assist me in any way.
> Sincerely,
> —TERRI

No matter how little information you have, take time to start a log or record with each name. See how much other information you can list pertaining to that name. Depending on the time period you are working with, perhaps there was a will or an estate involved. There may have been property, so a deed and tax records might exist at the state archives and library. All fifty-two states and territories in the United States have Web pages for their state libraries and archives. These are easy to reach by going to the USGenWebsite at www.usgenweb.org/ and then using the provided links to go to the appropriate state GenWebsite. Each state GenWebsite has a link to their state library and archives. Once you arrive at the state library and/or archive's Website, check for a list of the types of records available for the county where your ancestors lived. The USGenWeb project and the WorldGenWeb projects are free on-line genealogy projects for the benefit of the general public. They are maintained by an organized group of volunteers and do an excellent job of bringing together people and resources for tracing your family tree.

Once you have started your research log with all the pieces of information about your family, you will start to see what information you don't have about each ancestor. Most people find it helps them to stay focused if they work back chronologically documenting each ancestor's life from their death back to their birth (including something about their siblings) then on back to the next generation. Each time you add a new branch to your family tree you will want to survey what has been published in the past about that surname (last name) in that locality.

A good place to start your survey is on the Internet. The All-in-One Genealogy Search Page(s) (www.geocities.com/ Heartland/Acres/8310/gensearcher.html). This site allows you to search for your family names in a large number of databases on-line for free. It has collected in one location most of the best on-line genealogy databases like the Roots Surname List where almost 60,000 people have registered their research interests in more than 420,000 surnames worldwide. There is no charge for searching this database or for adding you surnames and research interests to the database. You can simply fill in the blanks in the supplied form on-line and sit back and wait for other researchers to contact you at your e-mail address.

The next step in tracing your family tree is with your birth certificate. I realize some people do not have one. Often the only record is the family Bible, because births and deaths were not recorded publicly until around the turn of the twentieth century. Church records and family Bibles also contain listings of baptisms, marriages, and deaths.

Original documents are the primary source of accurate genealogical information because they are records that were created at the time of important events in your ancestors' lives. For example, a local church or the local government may have recorded your ancestors' births, christenings/baptisms, marriages, and deaths/burials. In addition to civil and church records, original documents may also include census, military, immigration, land, and court records.

Dear Mrs. Tillman,

I have recently returned from Virginia. A friend there showed me a book that listed old Virginia families. There were many people on that list with my maiden name, which is an unusual one. My father's family is from Illinois, so I was surprised to find such a large group of them in Virginia. American history is a hobby of mine, and now I'm wondering if my family dates back to the American Revolution and the thirteen colonies. How can I find out?

I've enclosed a self-addressed, stamped envelope for any information you might have about tracing genealogies. Thanks.

Sincerely,

—NICOLE

Everyone wants to know something about his or her ancestry. All children, including adoptees and those living with their natural parents, have a difficult time forming their identity. The struggle is more complicated and fraught with anxiety for those whose ancestry is unknown to them. At some time or other, everyone asks the same questions: Who am I? Where did I come from? What makes me the way I am?

As you can see from the sample of letters I've received, people from many backgrounds want to know more about their families, their ancestors, and their cultural heritage. Whatever you know about yourself is your starting point. If you know who your parents are and where they were from, you can begin to search backward from there.

Once you have a record of your birth, use this information to look for your parents' birth records. If no birth records exist, there are other effective methods. There are many Websites where you can place free queries about your research interests. The USGenWeb project allows you to submit free queries that are automatically posted to the county GenWebsites. If you don't mind paying, you can also submit your queries to The Genealogy Helper published by Everton Publishers (www.everton.com). This magazine is one of the most widely circulated genealogy periodicals and can help you reach those who are not yet on the Internet. When writing a query, always remember to mention your ancestor by name and give at least one date and place where you can place that ancestor. For your query to be effective it must have these three pieces (a name, a date, and a place) whether published on paper or electronically on the Internet.

If your plan A does not work, don't worry; there is a plan B, a plan C, and maybe even a plan D. Searching for information may be time consuming, expensive, and frustrating, but eventually it is rewarding.

Remember my motto: Every problem contains the seed for the solution. All you have to do is learn to recognize the seed.

Genealogical research involves asking the following five basic questions over and over again:

1. What do I know about my family?
2. What do I want to learn about my family?
3. What records are available at the library?
4. What records are available on the Internet?
5. How do I obtain a record?
6. What do I do next?

Organize your records for easy access. Record your information on a chart and keep a research log of all records you locate. Make and file copies of key documents. If your survey fails to turn up published information about your ancestor, you then can do original research to fill in your family tree. Even if you do find something published about your ancestors during your survey, you may want to find original records to document those claims. Not everything in print on paper or on the Internet is accurate.

As you surf the Internet, it is good to have a starting point with links to different sites that can help you trace your family tree. Websites that organize thousands of links by category or topic are called directories.

Yahoo! is a directory and is one of the best known sites in the WorldWideWeb portion of the Internet. Yahoo! can help you if you don't quite know how to define what you are looking for in words. Its categories can give you ideas of other terms to use to find what you are seeking on the Internet.

Another Web directory specifically designed to help people trace their family trees is Cyndi's List of Genealogy Sites on the Internet (www.cyndislist.com/). This site has over thirty thousand links to Websites and even has a category called "Hit a Brick Wall?" with links to Websites that can help you overcome obstacles and dead ends in your research.

The World Wide Web contains many tools to help you determine what records exist that may have information about your ancestors. It can help you find a local library, archives, or LDS Family History Center that has a copy of those records. It can help you find your way with maps and travel directions to that institution to make your searches. It can even help you find reduced airfares and reserve a rental car or hotel room around the world (www.expedia.com and www.travelocity.com) as you travel to the places your ancestors lived to do on-location research.

In a few cases, you may even find digitized images of original documents on-line that you can use to document your ancestry. How exciting it is to search at midnight through an index of early Virginia land patents and find 400 acres in Kentucky surveyed by Daniel Boone for your ancestor. How nearly unbelievable it is to then download a digitized image of that 1786 land patent and enlarge it and print it on your computer at home.

The Internet will not research your family tree for you. The WorldWideWeb and the rest of the Internet only make the process of tracing your family tree easier and more convenient than ever before.

In genealogical research, you must evaluate each new piece of information and then decide where this information might lead you. One of the most valuable contacts is the county historian or the historical society of the community in which you are searching. The historical society primarily consists of people who are natives to the area and are knowledgeable about families who lived there. This is especially true of a small town in which the residents were not transient. Historians will know local private family cemeteries and who maintains them and their records. You can get a list of county historians at a public library or state archives. You can also find this information quickly and conveniently at that county's GenWebsite. From the USGenWebsite, choose a link to that state's GenWebsite. On the state's GenWebsite look for a link to that county's

GenWebsite. On the county GenWebsite, you will find much helpful information that usually includes how to contact the county historian and the local genealogical and historical societies for that area.

Once you have this list, you may want to write a letter, telephone, or visit the historian, requesting information about the family you are researching.

Here are a few more valuable sources for your genealogical search:

Birth Certificates and Death Records

On the Internet you can obtain detailed information on ordering vital records from each state in the United States. You can even download the official forms for each state for ordering copies of birth and death records. A shortcut to each state's information is found under "Vital Records Information" at the All-in-One Genealogy Search Page by GenSearcher (www. geocities.com/Heartland/Acres/8310/gensearcher.html).

The Bureau of the Census does not issue birth certificates, nor does it keep files or indexes of birth records. These are maintained by the Office of Vital Statistics in the states or areas where the births occurred.

The National Archives has records of births at U.S. Army facilities in the states and territories for 1884 to 1912, with some records dated as late as 1928. It will search the records if provided with: name of child, names of his/her parents, place of birth, and month and year of birth. Military Service Records in the National Archives of the United States has details. The leaflet is available free of charge from Publication Services, National Archives and Records Administration, Washington, DC 20408.

The value of death records is that they give the date of birth as well as the date of death, the place of birth, and the names of other family members. If you do not live in a city with a library, it may be possible to request a search by mail. Some libraries allow you to bring your own computer disk and download the information at no charge. Copies may cost only a dime or quarter. When requesting information by mail, always include a large, self-addressed, stamped envelop. When actually visiting a library, always bring lots of change for copies.

Another source for obtaining death records is through an information broker, who will have access to a computer network of all deaths (1940–1993) from the Social Security master death index. This index is also available on-line for free searches at the Ancestry.com Website (www.ancestry.com). This Website has many other biographical and genealogical databases for you to search on-line. Some are free, others require that you pay a fee as a subscribing member.

If you do not have the time or are unable to actually conduct your own genealogical search, you may prefer to hire a professional genealogical searcher. Some searches may take years and become quite expensive. The association of Professional Genealogists promotes professional standards among genealogists. Their Website includes their brochure titled "So You're Going to Hire a Professional Genealogist" (www.apgen.org/hire.htm) with helpful suggestions for those seeking professional help.

Census Records

Census records are released every ten years, but they must be seventy years old before they are made public. If you are searching for someone who was born prior to 1920, there is a good chance the family will be listed in the census of 1920 or earlier. The census lists all persons living in a household, even nonfamily members such as boarders or tenants. Census records are recorded on microfilm and are available at a state archives and library and often at a main public library.

Census schedules for 1790 through 1920 in the custody of the National Archives are distributed on microfilm to many libraries and other users and are open to the public. Title 44, U.S. Code, allows the public to use the National Archives' census record holdings after seventy-two years. The archives will not research census records, but will copy them (and provide certification, if necessary) for a fee, if given the exact volume and page citation.

The 1890 census is limited to fragments from Alabama, the District of Columbia, Georgia, Illinois, Minnesota, New Jersey, New York, North Carolina, Ohio, South Dakota, and Texas, in addition to the special 1890 schedules covering Union veterans of the Civil War and their widows.

There are federal decennial census schedules, other than for population and principally from the nineteenth century, that contain some information about individuals or their activities and living conditions. These records deal with agriculture, manufacturing, mining, mortality, and such social concerns as schools, libraries, and wages. The National Archives has some of these records on microfilm; others are in collections in state archives.

Since the Bureau of the Census was established as a permanent organization in 1902, it has had continual requests for information from individuals interested in history and genealogy and for certified transcripts of census records for use in court proceedings and for other purposes. Many states did not register births until after 1900 and some still did not begin such documentation until the late 1920s. Civil War veterans were among the first to need census transcripts (showing their ages) to support their pension claims.

Legislation affecting employment of children, various states' pension laws, mobilization of men and women for defense employment in which proof of citizenship was required, and the need to prove age and citizenship to travel abroad all increased the volume of requests for personal information recorded in the census.

The Bureau of the Census formed a special searching section in the late 1920s. After the national Social Security law was enacted in 1936, demands for help from people who found they had to have evidence of their age and had nowhere else to turn increased from 60,000 in 1937 to more than 700,000 a year during World War II. Because of the need for additional space, the searching section (now named the Personal Census Service Branch) moved to Pittsburg, Kansas, in August 1958. The present volume of age search requests runs about 50,000 a year.

The United States was the first nation to write census-taking into its constitution (Article I, Section 2) and in doing so to create a series of statistical records about its people. In 1790, and every ten years since then, a federal population census has told how many persons there were in a certain age group, of a particular race, male or female, and so on. The "manuscript census schedules," as they are called, at first showed only the name of each family head, but added later was the name of every individual (to make certain no one was missed or counted twice), together with data about that household or person. Some of the schedules were subsequently lost or burned, such as in the War of 1812. Most of the remaining ones, and those collected in later years, were bound into volumes and stored. Most of the 1890 schedules were lost in a fire in 1921. Beginning in the 1920s, all remaining schedules were microfilmed. The originals that were open to the public were offered to state and other archives, such as the Daughters of the American Revolution, or were destroyed by congressional order to save space.

Thus the federal population censuses are a major source of information about individuals over spans of years and generations. Some of this information is available to the public, but most is deemed confidential by law.

The exact questions asked in each of the censuses, together with the enumerators' instructions, appear in a U.S. Bureau of the Census publication, *200 Years of U.S. Census Taking: Population and Housing Questions, 1790–1990* (Washington DC, Government Printing Office, 1989).

Although a population census has been taken in the United States every ten years since 1790, the bureau holds only the records for 1900 through 1990. The Personal Census Service Branch (PCSB), in Pittsburg, Kansas, maintains and searches these records, which are confidential by law. Information from them is available only to the named individuals, their heirs, or legal representatives. The PCSB also will tabulate (on a reimbursable basis) statistics not already published in census reports. This is done in such a way that no individual or household can be identified.

Census records are on microfilm and are arranged by geographic location—state, county, place, enumeration district (ED), ward, and the like. Within these, a street address may appear in urban areas. The listings on the record pages are in the order of the census-takers' house-to-house visits or, in recent years, the addresses to which census questionnaires were sent by mail. Thus an address—or in the case of a rural location, the distance and direction from a known place—is needed to find a record. There are ED maps for all states from 1930 on, with some for previous censuses dating back to 1880. There also are indexes to street addresses arranged by EDs on microfilm and microfiche for some years. (The National Archives has maps and address indexes available for public use and sale.) The Pittsburg staff also maintains a library of city directories, alphabetic indexes, and a special index file called Soundex, which groups together surnames of the same or similar sounds but of variant spellings.

The Bureau of the Census does not make any distinction on its questionnaires between natural or adopted children.

There are microfilm indexes for 1880 (all states and territories, but only for households with children), 1900, 1910 (twenty-one states, principally those in the South), 1920, and 1930 (partial). The National Archives has 1880, 1900, and 1910 indexes, which are available to the public. (The Bureau of the Census has indexes for 1900 through 1930, but only for internal use.)

In addition, there are ongoing projects to compile alphabetical indexes to the federal population census records. Some may cover entire states; others are only for certain counties and particular years. Any checklist of these indexes would be incomplete, but researchers may wish to consult the latest edition of *Genealogical and Local History Books in Print* (three volumes, paperback, $32.50), where such indexes are listed. Most county GenWebsites include information with the availability of indexed census records for that county.

Cyndi's List of Genealogy Sites on the Internet (www.cyndislist.com/) includes categories for Census Related Sites Worldwide, U.S. Census, and the U.S. National Archives. The National Archives and Records Administration has a Website with information and census records and passenger lists (gopher.nara.gov/). They also have on microfilm all of the available census schedules (1790–1920) and the indexes to those for 1880, 1900, and 1910. Copies are available at a moderate cost per roll of film. The archives' publications—*Federal Population Censuses, 1790–1890, 1900; Federal Population Census;* and the *1910 Federal Population Census*—contain roll listings and indicate the price for each roll. They will be mailed on request. Direct inquiries to:

Publication Orders
National Archives and Records
Administration
7th & Pennsylvania Ave., NW
Washington, DC 20408
(202) 523-3181

> *Knowing one's identity is vital to
> human development.*

These microfilmed census schedules are also available for use in reference rooms at the National Archives and Records

Administration, Reference Service Branch (NNRM), and at the archives' regional branches (check the list in the Reference Section). These branches also have copy facilities for their patrons and at some locations provide a request for information form, which may be mailed.

Copies (certified, if requested) of specifically identified pages of the federal population schedules may be ordered from the National Archives' headquarters. Provide the name of the individual listed, page number, census year, state and county; and for the 1880 through 1920 censuses, the enumeration district.

Many public and academic libraries, state archives, and historical and genealogical societies have reference collections of census microfilm. Most local libraries have lists of such sources; the principal one is Federal Population and Mortality Schedules, 1790–1920, in the National Archives and the States, Special List Number 24 (microfiche) (National Archives and Records Administration, 1986).

Individual users also may borrow the microfilm through some libraries and research institutions. Microfilm rolls of 1790 to 1910 population schedules also can be rented directly by contacting:

Census Microfilm Program
P. O. Box 30
Annapolis Junction, MD 20701-0030
(301) 604-3699

Within political boundaries, such as counties and cities, census records often are arranged by ED number. Beginning in 1880, some enumerators carried ED maps that showed their census assignments—prior to that, their assigned areas were simply described in their commissions—and they marked the houses and routes on them. The National Archives' Cartographic and Architectural Branch, in Alexandria, Virginia, has a collection of these maps. The archives produced indexes on microfilm or microfiche that relate street address ranges to enumeration districts for some census years.

Some states took their own censuses after the year 1790 to serve constitutional provisions for apportioning representatives to their legislatures. Territorial censuses were taken by territorial organizations and usually represented attempts to establish eligibility for admission into the Union as a state. These records are in the custody of the secretary of state in the state in which the census was taken.

The 1920 census is the most recent record released. However, all states may not be indexed. In some states your research must begin with the 1900 census, which is indexed for all states.

You must know at least your ancestor's full name and state or territory of residence to begin research in the 1900, 1910, or 1920 census. Although not absolutely necessary, it is helpful to know the full name of the head of the household in which your ancestor lived. It is possible to search with a surname only, but because it involves the process of elimination, it takes longer.

The Library of Congress has cadastral and fire maps that may be useful in pinpointing the locations of households listed in the censuses.

Family tree books are available, however, unless you have a rare surname, these types of books are not helpful at all and can be a rip-off. While many legitimate family history books have been written, the field of genealogy is plagued with offers sent via the U.S. Postal service to sell you "the" book about your name for thirty to forty dollars. These types of books usually turn out to be not much more than a short discourse on the historical origins of that surname and copies of information found in telephone books for people with that surname. The gross facts are that if you're researching the surname Gross your ancestors may have come from Germany, but they also may have come from France or the U.K. or any number of other countries. Without methodical research documenting each generation, you'll never know for sure. If you should be taken in by such a scam see the National Genealogical Society's Website (www.ngsgenealogy.org/) and click on "About NGS" then click on "Committees" and finally click on "Consumer Protection" for some sound advice.

Subscribe to *Everton's Genealogical Helper*. It is a standard reference tool especially for queries. Everton's has a useful Website (www.everton.com) full of helpful information.

Immigration and Naturalization Records

With the exception of Native Americans, all of us have forefathers who immigrated to this country. There is a computer situated on Ellis Island in New York City that has a record of many immigrants who arrived in that port. There are also excellent records available at most National Archives branches of many passenger lists of ships arriving in the United States. Passenger lists contain the following information: passenger's name, age, race, sex, occupation, and marital status; name and address of nearest foreign relative; last residence; port of arrival; and final destination.

This information is kept on microfilm at the National Archives. To obtain microfilm data about a particular immigrant, request several original copies of NATF Form 81, "Order for Copies of Ship and Passenger Arrival Records." A small fee is charged when the information is located.

If you have reason to believe that the person you are looking for may have been an immigrant, two types of citizenship records will be available: documentation of becoming a U.S. citizen and naturalization records. The latter usually include declaration of intention, a petition, and a certificate of naturalization.

Three separate sets of these records are issued for every new citizen who entered the United States after 1906. One copy is given to the citizen. The second is filed with the court of jurisdiction, usually in the county where the individual first established residency. The third copy is retained by the U.S. Immigration and Naturalization Service (INS). These records typically include name and address of applicant, nationality and country of immigration, age and or birthdate, marital status, and names of spouse and children.

Write to:
>
> Immigration and Naturalization Service (INS)
> (www.ins.usdoj.gov)
> U.S. Dept. of Justice
> 425 I Street NW
> Washington, DC 20536

To obtain a copy of the birth certificate of a U.S. citizen in a foreign country, request an original Form FS-240 from:
>
> Passport Services
> (www.travel.state.gov)
> Correspondence Branch
> U.S. Dept. of State
> Washington, DC 20007

If you are looking for a death record of a U.S. citizen who died in a foreign country, write to the above address for Passport Services and request an original Form OF-180, "Report of the Death of an American Citizen Abroad."

The National Archives offers the catalog Immigrant and Passenger Arrivals. If your local library does not have a copy, send a $2 money order to:
>
> Catalog
> Dept. G05
> National Archives
> (www.archives.ca/www/svcs/english/Genealogy.html)
> Washington, DC 20408

This catalog indexes reels of microfilm in an easily understood format. Reels can be purchased for $23 each. Check with your local library and/or Mormon Family History Center to see which reels are available locally.

The Civil Reference Branch (NNRC) of the National Archives has passenger arrival lists and immigration passenger lists. These lists may also be found in the reference sections of many other libraries. The MOT (Marine Ocean Terminal), Building 22, Bayonne, NJ 07002-5388, (201) 823-7252, has a form by which a request for information may be submitted by mail.

Libraries

Most large libraries today (from the Library of Congress to city libraries) have at least part of their collections electronically catalogued. These large libraries usually have a Website where you can search their electronic catalogs on-line at your convenience. Not only do library catalogs on-line often give you the call number of the book or microfilm you may want to look in, but many electronic catalogs also tell you if that book is currently checked out.

As you begin to survey what has been published, don't forget to search on-line at the libraries closest to you for county history books and family history books that may contain information about your ancestors. Each library's Website can provide you with other useful information. Typically such a Website will list that library's address, operating hours, where to find parking nearby, and if you are lucky the locations and costs for making copies of what you may find in that library.

The best genealogical library belongs to the Church of Jesus Christ of Latter-day Saints in Salt Lake City, Utah. Since its beginning in 1894, the main library has become the largest of its kind in the world. It has a collection of more than 1 million rolls of microfilm, 150,000 books, 8 million family records, and many other records. Go to the LDS Family History Center's Website (www.lds.org/Family_History/Where_is.html) to locate the branch nearest you.

Their catalog is available on computer at their main library in Salt Lake City and on microfiche and/or computer CDs at their branch Family History Centers around the world. there is no charge to use any of the LDS Family History Centers around the world or the main Family History Library in Salt Lake City. You will, however, be asked to pay for any copies you make at those facilities. There is a small shipping charge (and local tax where applicable) if you request that rolls of microfilm or sheets of microfiche be sent from the main Family History Library to a branch Family History Center. Books (there are a few restricted records on microfilm or microfiche that do not circulate from Salt Lake City to the branches).

The LDS (Mormon) Church also publishes the FamilySearch computer system that includes several large databases with information on more than 284 million deceased persons (most of whom died before 1900). The FamilySearch system is available on computers at the Family History Library and FamilySearch Center in downtown Salt Lake City, at all of the branch LDS Family History Centers worldwide, and at many large libraries with genealogical collections in the United States. There is no charge for using FamilySearch other than a very small fee for printouts of information found in these computer databases.

Most of the main library's records have been acquired through an extensive microfilming program started in 1938. At present, more than one hundred microfilmers are filming original documents in courthouses, churches, and other archives throughout the world. The microfilmers send the rolls of film to Salt Lake City where they are preserved in a vault in the mountains nearby. Microfilm copies can be ordered and sent to a branch library in your area.

Workers in the branch libraries are volunteers who can help you order and use the main library's records. They can't do research for you, but they can assist you with your own research. Call ahead to determine the library's schedule and to inquire whether you need to reserve a microfilm reader.

Updated catalogs and indexes on microfilm and microfiche are available to help you search for your ancestors. There are also reference aids, research papers, and other related publications. SourceGuide on CD from the LDS Church Distribution Center contains most of the reference aids and research papers mentioned in this paragraph (to order a CD call 800-537-5950).

Native American Ancestry

The census schedules for 1860 through 1920 and many other records concerning Native Americans, chiefly those who maintained their tribal status, are available to the public at the Civil Reference Branch of the National Archives, archives' regional branches, and at some libraries in various parts of the country. Also available at the National Archives and on microfilm are the Native American census rolls, 1885 to 1940. For detailed holdings, see *American Indians, A Select Catalog of National Archives Microfilm Publications* (National Archives Trust Fund Board, 1984) and *Guide to Genealogical Research in the National Archives* (National Archives Trust Fund Board, 1982).

The Tribal Affairs Division (U.S. Bureau of Indian Affairs, Washington, DC 20245) will not provide lists of names, but will search its records for verification of Native American ancestry if given the tribe's specific name, name of the person, and date and place of birth.

A word of warning. Tracing your family tree (a.k.a. doing genealogy) is addictive. Many people have set out to find just a little bit of information about their family tree and find themselves spending years tracing their roots. Not all your living family members may end up sharing your enthusiasm for chasing dead ancestors. Here again the Internet can help you. The Internet can help you find a genealogical society in your area (even if your ancestors did not live where you now live). For a small annual membership fee you can join your local genealogical society and attend regular (usually monthly) lectures and beginners classes. Your local genealogical society may even have a computer interest group where you can learn to use genealogy software (to organize all the information you have found out about your family tree) and to more fully use the Internet.

15

Reference Section

A Note from Norma

This chapter may be the most important, most useful, most valuable part of the entire text!

The preceding chapters are built around a single theme—searches for mothers, fathers, children, or other specific cases. In this reference section, you'll find names, addresses, suggestions, and options for further investigation. They could apply to virtually any search; when combined with other information, they may lead you to the person you've been seeking and to that reunion you've been dreaming about.

I hope you'll find your search as exciting as a treasure hunt or a real-life mystery adventure. And if you're missing some clues, you just may find them in the pages that follow.

Finding a missing person is an awesome experience, one that can forever change your life by filling a void and making you feel complete. At last you can put a closure to living with the unknown and have peace of mind. I know that many of you are afraid of what you might find. Let me assure you that what you find is better than not knowing, even if it is not what you hoped for.

As you embark on your search, I urge you to think positively and be persistent—don't give up or get discouraged. Have realistic expectations and be prepared to accept whatever you find.

183

Don't procrastinate. There is no time better than now to begin. I know you can do it. Don't fear the unknown and don't be afraid of the truth.

Once your search is completed, you might even consider helping another person with his or her search. I'm living proof that searching can become addictive! Helping someone find a missing loved one is one of the most challenging and rewarding experiences in the world.

When your search is complete, write me a letter and tell me all about it. Please send me a picture of you and your loved one. I wish I could be there for your reunion.

Best wishes for your successful search and reunion.

CHECKLIST

	Fill in responses here
Legal and proper name (full first, middle, and last) • possible surname search • possible "Super Search" product	
Height, weight, color of hair, color of eyes, family information, etc.	
Last and all know telephone numbers • possible crisscross search	
Social Security number • possible credit "header" search	
All addresses (current or last known) • possible address update on-line search if within the last seven years • "Super Search product	
Current and all known employment (name, address, and telephone number) • possible telephone call to human resource department	
Driver's license or automobile license • possible on-line DMV search by state	
Relatives/Friends • possible telephone call as long-lost friend	
Schools (start with most recently attended) • possible telephone call to alumni association or admissions department	
Business connections • on-line business search, numerous products	
State professional licenses • on-line search/telephone call to the state's licensing bureau	
Former or current military • possible contact with U.S. government	
Credit information • only with suject's approval or when legal, consult attorney	
Association memberships • possible telephone to association	
Date of birth • possible check of county criminal information or drivers check by state	

(Fill out a separate form for each subject.)

WHERE TO LOOK FOR ADDITIONAL INFORMATION

LOCAL RECORDS

COURTHOUSE

Marriage	Probate (Wills)	Liens
Divorce	Registrar of deeds	Criminal
Voters	Judgments	Business licenses
Property owners	Lawsuits	Adoption records
Assessors		

Ask where old records are stored. There may be a local archives.

PUBLIC LIBRARY REFERENCE SECTION

Obituaries/death notices	Telephone directories
School yearbooks	Genealogy reference materials
City/suburban directories	Birth records
Crisscross directories	Census records
Microfilm/microfiche/CD-ROM	Old newspapers/periodicals

State room (Almost every state has a library with a room devoted to state historical information.)

STATE RECORDS

Birth certificates	Military enlistments/discharges
Death certificates	Adoption records
Marriage records	Professional licenses
Driving records	Corporation records
Vehicle registration	

STATE ARCHIVES

Census records	Old telephone directories
Birth index	Genealogical records
Military records	Immigration passenger lists
Military enlistments/discharge	Microfilm/microfiche
Old newspapers	Old county courthouse records
Old city/suburban directories	Adoption records
Old yearbooks	

FEDERAL RECORDS & RESOURCES

Military records	National Archives & branches
Social Security master death index	Offices of Disclosure
Bankruptcy records	IRS
Veterans' Administration	Social Security
Military Locating Services	Immigration & Naturalization Office

OTHER RECORDS

Family Bibles	
Family genealogical records	Church records & directories
Mormon Church libraries	Membership
Genealogists	Baptismal/marriage/death
Everton's Genealogical Helper	Cemetery & funeral home records
School records	Veterans' organizations
Civic organizations	Embassies of other countries
Professional associations	Adoption search & support groups
Historical society	Adoption agencies
County historian	Adoption records/social workers
Family cemeteries	

*Not all records are available in every state.

National Archives and Regional Branches

National Archives Headquarters
7th & Pennsylvania Ave. NW
Washington, DC 20408
(202) 501-5400

National Archives/Northwest
   Region
6125 Sand Point Way, NE
Seattle, WA 98115
(206) 526-6507

National Archives/New England
   Region
380 Trapelo Rd.
Waltham, MA 02154
(617) 647-8100

National Archives/Alaska
654 W. 3rd Ave.
Anchorage, AK 99501
(907) 271-2441

National Archives/Pacific
   Southwest
P.O. Box 25307
Laguna Niguel, CA 92677
(303) 236-0817

National Archives/Mountain
   States
24000 Avila Rd.
Denver, CO 80225
(714) 643-4241

National Archives/Pacific Sierra
1000 Commodore Dr.
San Bruno, CA 94066
(415) 876-9009

National Archives/Central Plains
2312 E. Bannister Rd.
Kansas City, MO 64131
(816) 026-6272

National Archives/Southwest/Gulf
   Region
P.O. Box 6216
Fort Worth, TX 76115
(817) 334-5525

National Archives/Southeast
   Region
1557 St. Joseph Ave.
East Point, GA 30344
(404) 763-7477

National Archives/Great Lakes
   Region
7358 S. Pulaski Rd.
Chicago, IL 60629
(312) 581-7816

National Archives/Northeast
   Region
Building #22
MOT (Marine Ocean Terminal),
   Bayonne
Bayonne, NJ 07002
(201) 823-7545

National Archives/Mid-Atlantic
   Region
9th & Market Sts.
Room 1350
Philadelphia, PA 19107
(215) 597-3000

Federal Agencies

Here are some federal agencies that might be sources of information in your search:

Congress:
    House: ....(202) 225-3121
    Senate: ....(202) 224-3121

Department of Commerce:..(202) 377-2000

Department of Defense (all military brances):...................(202) 545-6700

Department of Justice:..(202) 514-2000

Inmate Monitoring Serviece: ....(202) 307-3036

Inmate Locating Service: ....(202) 307-3126

Drug Registration: ....(202)267-3484

Aircraft Registration and Pilot Certification:...................(405) 680-3205

Federal Election Commission:...(202) 219-3420
    (800) 424-9530

General Services Administration:.......................................(202) 535-0800

Interpol (International Child Abduction):........................(202) 272-8383

Library of Congress:...(202) 707-5000

National Reference:..(202) 707-5522

Military Locators (active):
    Air Force: ....(512) 652-5774
    Navy:...(703) 614-3155
    Army: ....(317) 542-4211
    Marines: ....(703) 640-3942

Military Personnel Records (all branches):.......................(314) 263-3901

National Archives: ....(202) 501-5402

National Center for Missing & Exploited Children: ....(800) 843-5678

National Institute of Standards & Technology:.................(301) 975-2000

National Ocean & Atmospheric Administration:.............(301) 443-8330

National Transportation Safety Board: ....(202) 382-6600

U.S. Coast Guard Locators:
    Active: ....(202) 267-1615
    Reserves: ....(202) 267-0547
    Retired: ....(202) 267-0546

U.S. Department of State (country desks):.........................(202) 647-4000

U.S. Merchant Marine Locators

(U.S. Coast Guard): ....(202) 267-4000

U.S. Patrent & Trademark Office: ....(202) 557-5168

Veterans' Pension Information:..(202) 233-2044

White House (liaison):...(202) 456-7486

For catalog information write:

Consumer Information Center,
    P.O. Box 100
    Pueblo, CO 81002 ....(719) 948-3334

Information USA,
    P.O. Box 15700
    Chevy Chase, MD 20815 ....(301) 657-1200

Congressional Gov't Judiciary

    Mt. Vernon, VA 22121...(703) 765-3400

Superintendent of Documents

U.S. Government Printing Office,
    N. Captiol & H Street, NW
    Washington, DC 20402...(202) 275-2051

Washington Researchers,
    2612 P Street, NW
    Washington, DC 20007...(202) 333-3499

Helpful Websites

Adoption

Adoption search and support groups exchange information and maintain support for their members. For an updated list of adoption groups be sure to check www.reunion.com. Here is a list of a few Websites that I found on the Internet.

Adopted Child:..*www.raisingadoptedchildren.com*

American Adoption Congress (AAC): ....*www.rdz.stjohns.edu*

Concerned United Birthparents (CUB):........................*www.webnations.com/cub*

Midwest Adoption Center: ....*www.members.aol.com/macadopt*

National Adoption Information Clearinghouse (NAIC): ....*www.calib.com/naic*

Search Connection:..*www.infind4u.com*

Truth Seekers in Adoption: ....*www.wbrn.com/truthseekers*

Worldwide Tracers:...*www.worldwidetracers.com*

Registry:...................................*www.reunion.com*...............active adoption searches

Search Ads: ....*www.reunion.com/adoption.htm* ....active adoption searches

Searcher:..........................*www.cfinvestigations.com* ....active adoption searches

Deadbeats

Baby Bag:............................*www.babybag.com* ....bulletin boards

Support Kids: ....*www.supportkids.com* ....collections

Directories

Area Codes: ..*gopher://odie.niaid.nih.gov/77/deskref/.areacode/indes*............area code database

Big Book:................................*www.bigbook.com*..........U.S. businesses on the Web

Bureau of Prisons: ....*www.bop.gov*.................nationwide list of prisons

U.S. Post Office: ....*www.usps.gov*....................addresses and zip codes

Embassy Page:........................*www.embpage.org* .... phone numbers/ e-mail addresses

Federal Government

Agencies: ....*www.lib.lsu.edu/gov/fedgov.html* ....directory

Four11 People Finder:............*www.four11.com*.......e-mail address of on-line users

Government Agencies:

www.yahoo.com/Government/U_S_Government/Agencies/Independent ....government agency Websites

Info Space: ....*www.infospace.com* ...international telephone/e-mail directories

Internet Address Finder: ....*www.iaf.net* ....e-mail directory

Info USA: ....*www.abii.com* ....phone directories

National Address Server: ...*www.cedar.buffalo.edu*..................addresses plus zip+4.
NCIN—National
Credit Information: ....*www.reunion.com* ....3 billion records
   Locator: ....*www.cenuiuc.edu/cgi-bin/find-news* ....newsgroup directory
   Dejanews: ....*www.dejanews.com*....................newsgroup directory
   Tilenet: ....*www.tile.net*...directories
Reference.com: ....*www.reference.com* ....newsgroups and forums
Federal Government: ....*www.clip.org* ....links for Federal
                                                 government Websites
State Government Websites: ....*www.states.org* ....directory
State Libraries:
   sunsite.berkeley.edu/Libweb/usa-state.html...........................links to state libraries
Telephone Directories: ....*www.networkx.com*.......................................directory
555-1212: ....*www.555-1212.com* ....e-mail addresses/phone
                                               numbers/Websites
Switchboard: ....*www.switchboard.com* ....phone numbers
WhoWhere: ....*www.whowhere.com* ....e-mail/addresses/phone
                                               numbers/Websites

Genealogy

Ancestors: ....*www.ancestry.com* ....genealogy database
Bureau of Census: ....*govinfo.kerr.orst.edu/usaco-sttis.html*..........census information
Everton's: ....*www.everton's.com*......................genealogy magazine
Family Tree Maker:
   www.familytreemaker.com/00000229.html......................genealogy software
Genealogy: ....*www.ancestry.com* ....genealogy database
Genealogy Links: ....*www.reunion.com*..........links to genealogy Websites

Locating Services

California Information
Specialist: ....*www.cfinvestigations.com*........C. F. Investigations (Fee)
Nationwide Locating
Service: ....*www.nationwidelocate.com*..........information broker and
                                              locating service (Fee)
Missing Persons Magazine
and Registry: ....*www.reunion.com* ....registry and classified ads
                                            for missing persons (Fee)
Social Security: ....*www.ssa.gov*..... forwarding a letter to next of kin

Maps

Mapquest: ....*www.mapquest.com* ....insert address
                                             to get a street map

411 Locate:............................*www.411locate.com*......................maps and addresses

Military

Military Locating

Services:................................*www.militarycity.com*...............military searches (Fee)

Air Force: ....*www.afpc.af.mil*...........................Active duty only

Army:......................................*www.army.mil*.............................Active duty only

Military Reunions &

Searches: ....*www.reunion.com/military.htm*.......................classified ads

Research

Death Claims: ....*www.infobases.com*..........................free death search

Finger: ....*www.emailman.com/finger*...............find somone on-line
right now

Library of Congress:..................*www.loc.gov*.....................................research tools

Missing Persons Magazine: ....*www.reunion.com*...................................classified ads
and personal messages (Fee)

People Finder:......................*www.home.netscape.com*.....find people on the Internet

P.I. Magazine: ....*www.pimall.com*...........professional magazine about
private investigators

Privacy Act: ....*www.livelinks.com/sumeria/politics/foia.html*..................laws about
restricted records

Public Records: ....*www.brbpub.com*.........................free public records

State Unclaimed Property:........*unclaimed.org*.............locating unclaimed property

Vital Records: ....*www.inlink.com*......................foreign and domestic
vital records

Search Engines

Alta Vista: ....*www.altavista.digital.com*...........................search engine

AOL Netfind: ....*www.aol.com/netfind/business.html*...................search engine

Big Foot:.................................*www.bigfoot.com*...............................search engine

Infoseek: ....*www.infoseek.com*...............................search engine

Lycos: ....*www.lycos.com*.................................search engine

Our World:......................*ourworld.compuserve.com*..........................search engine

Starting Point:...........................*www.stpt.com*...................................search engine

Switchboard.com:...............*www.switchboard.com*.............................search engine

Webcrawler:.........................*www.webcrawler.com*...............................search engine

Yahoo People Search:..............*www.yahoo.com*...............................search engine

Information Brokers

A Matter of Fact
2976 Camargo Court
San Jose, CA 95132
(408) 926-2125

Access Information Services
1323 Twenty-sixth Avenue
San Francisco, CA 94122
(415) 564-9096

Alex Kramer
1757 Lamont Street, NW
Washington, DC 20010

Automated Data Retrieval
    Services
8934 Lakewood Drive, Suite 274
Windsor, CA 95492
(800) 270-2377

Ayers Information Network
3545 Indian Queen Lane
Philadelphia, PA 19129-1539
(215) 842-9450

Background America
1900 Church Street #400
Nashville, TN 37203
(800) 697-7189
www.background-us.com

Berinstein Research
5070 Campo Road
Woodland Hills, CA 91364
(818) 704-6460

Burana Consulting and Research
PO Box 1752
Lake Arrowhead, CA 92352
(909) 337-1484

Burwell Enterprises
3724 F.M. 1960 West, Suite 214
Houston, TX 77068
(713) 537-9051

Cal Info
1957 North Bronson #101
Los Angeles, CA 90068
(213) 957-5035

CARCO Group Inc.
17 Flowerfield Industrial Park
St. James, NY 11780
(516) 584-7094

CDB InfoTek
6 Hutton Centre
Santa Ana, CA 92707
(800) 427-3747

CCH Incorporated
2700 Lake Cook Road
Riverwoods, IL 60015
(847) 267-7000

CK Research Associates
7570 Skillman #112
Dallas, TX 75231
(214) 503-7305

Chemcomm Corporation
PO Box 11206
Alexandria, VA 22312
(703) 998-4566

Clark Boardman Callaghan
375 Hudson Street
New York, NY 10014
(212) 924-7500

Competitive Analysis
Technologies
11702-B Grant, Suite 112
Cypress, TX 77429
(713) 370-3846

Compton Research Services
PO Box 15895
Rio Rancho, NM 87174
(505) 899-2975

Continental Commercial Advisors
522 Twenty-fifth Street
Santa Monica, CA 90402
(310) 395-7027

Cooper Hydock Rugge, Inc.
622 S Forty-second Street
Philadelphia, PA 19104
(215) 823-5490

Cooper Information
5 Ellery Place
Cambridge, MA 01238
(617) 354-3274

Computer Assisted Research On
Line
1166 NE 182nd Street
Miami, FL 33162
(800) 329-6397

Confi-check Investigations
1507 Twenty-fourth Street
Sacramento, CA 95816
(800) 921-7404

C.V.P. Services
13613 Country Lane
Burnsville, MN 55337
(612) 435-7986

DAC Services
(800) 331-9175
www.dacservices.com

Deward Houck & Associates
PO Box 1185
Lakeside, CA 92040
(619) 390-7291

Dun & Bradstreet Information
Services
3 Sylvan Way
Parsippany, NJ 07054
(800) 234-3867
Fax: (512) 794-7670
www.dbisna.com

Fact or Fiction Research
240 South Grand Oaks Avenue
Pasadena, CA 91107
(818) 577-9311

FINDS/SVP, Inc.
625 Avenue of the Americas
New York, NY 10011
(212) 645-4500

Financial Investigative Services,
Ltd.
PO Box 301
Augusta, ME 04332
(207) 622-5674

Fourth Wave, Inc.
PO Box 6547
Alexandria, VA 22306
(703) 360-4800

Franklin Information Group
4120 West Maplecrest Drive
Franklin, WI 53132
(414) 761-8771

FYI/Services
Box 84 Wittenberg Road
Bearsville, NY 12409
(914) 679-4815

Golden Information Group
753 N Thirty-fifth Street, Suite
312
Seattle, WA 98103
(206) 547-5662

Honolulu Information Service
PO Box 10447
Honolulu, HI 96816
(808) 733-2058

Infocite
8300 Chamberlin
Dexter, MI 48130-9327
(313) 426-4456

Information Edge
PO Box 373229
Satellite Beach, FL 32937
(407) 779-9161

Information Factory
Bayside 1001 Alternate A1A
Jupiter, FL 33477
(407) 622-1949

Information Matters
148 Hazel Drive
New Orleans, LA 70123
(504) 738-0070

Information Research Center
103 Five Oaks
San Antonio, TX 78209
(210) 829-0001

InfoSmith Research Services
107 S Mary Avenue, Suite 98
Sunnyvale, CA 94086
(408) 736-1107

Infotech Information & Research
11282 Washington Boulevard
Culver City, CA 90230
(310) 398-2568

InfoWorks
2033 Clement Avenue, Suite 222
Alameda, CA 94501-1317
(510) 865-8087

Intelligence Network, Inc.
PO Box 727
Clearwater, FL 34617
(800) 562-4007

International Research Center
PO Box 825
Tempe, AZ 85281
(602) 470-0389

1FM Data Services
951-2 Old Country Road, Suite
311
Belmont, CA 94002
(415) 570-5742

IQ Data
1401 El Camino, Suite 220
Sacramento, CA 98515
(800) 264-6517
www.iqdata.com

I.R.I.S.
2859 Galahad Drive NE
Atlanta, GA 30345-9459
(404) 321-9459

IRSC, Inc.
3777 N Harbor Boulevard
Fullerton, CA 92835
(800) 640-4772
Fax: (714) 738-9106
www.irsc.com

JAL Data Research Service
1110 Capitol Way South
Olympia, WA 98501
(360) 357-7040

Krauss Research
6114 LaSalle Avenue, Suite 413
Oakland, CA 94611
(510) 482-8760

Knowledge Access International
2685 Marine Way, Suite 1305
Mountain View, CA 94043
(415) 969-0606

Law Library Management, Inc.
38 Bunker Hill Drive
Huntington, NY 11743
(516) 266-1093

Lawquest, Inc.
PO Box 342
Fanwood, NJ 07023
(908) 322-8489

LegalEase, Inc.
139 Fulton Street, #1013
New York, NY 10038
(212) 393-9070

Lexis-Nexus
9393 Springboro Pike
PO Box 933
Dayton, OH 45401
(800) 227-9597

Library Specialists, Inc.
1000 Johnson Ferry Road, Suite
G1000
Marietta, GA 30068
(770) 578-6200

Longheed Resource Group, Inc.
2704 Rew Circle, Suite 102
Ocoee, FL 34761
(407) 654-1212

McBride and Associate, PI
1124 Second Street
Old Sacramento, CA 95814
(800) 995-9443
(a favorite of former law enforcement officers)

McComb Enterprises, Inc.
4144 W Lake Road
Canandaigua, NY 14424
(716) 394-7350

Multi/Data Briefing Service
PO Box 94444
Birmingham, AL 35220-4444
(205) 856-1101

NorthWest Online
2817 East Main Avenue
Puyallup, WA 98372
(206) 848-7767
www.nwlocation.com

OPEN (Ohio Professional
Electronic Network)
1650 Lake Shore Drive, Suite 180
Colombus, OH 43204
(614) 481-6999

Online Resources, Inc.
200 Little Falls Street, #G-201
Falls Church, VA 22046
(800) 678-9393

Pallorium, Inc.
PO Box 155—Midwood Station
Brooklyn, NY 11230
(212) 969-0286

PFC Information Services
6114 La Salle Avenue #149
Oakland, CA 94611
(510) 653-0666

Pinkerton Services Group
6100 Fairview Road, Suite 900
Charlotte, NC 27210
(800) 582-5745
www.worklife.com/pinkertn.htm

Research Data Service
9030 West Sahara Avenue #270
The Lakes, NV 89117
(702) 733-4990

Saporito & Associates
101 Murray Street
New York, NY 10007-2132
(212) 693-3474

Search International, Inc.
1870 N Roselle Road, Suite 105
Schaumburg, IL 60195
(708) 885-1950

Silver Birch Enterprises
1310 Maple Avenue, Suite 3C
Evanston, IL 60201-4325
(708) 864-4494

Snoop With The Scoop
PO Box 32790
San Jose, CA 95152-2770
(408) 258-1272

Steven Youmans & Associates
PO Box 6704
Ventura, CA 93006-6704
(213) 489-2208

Sullivan & Associates
182 Oleander Drive
San Rafael, CA 94903
(415) 472-2145

TechnoSearch Inc.
3915 Mission Avenue, #7-109
Oceanside, CA 92054
(619) 721-5500

Trans Union
1390 Willow Pass Road, Suite 620
Concord, CA 94520
(510) 689-1912 or (800) 899-7132
(they sell credit headers)

TRW REDI Property Data
844 Folsom Street #207
San Francisco, CA 94107-1123
(415) 543-6710

Vista Information Solutions, Inc.
55 Madison Avenue
Morristown, NJ 07960-7397
(201) 984-0666

State Offices
www.state.org

ALABAMA-
alaweb.asc.edu/agency.html

Department of Motor Vehicles:
Title Section
2721 Gunter Park Drive
PO Box 1331
Montgomery, AL 36102

Drivers License:
Drivers License Division
Certificate Section
PO Box 1471
Montgomery, AL 36102
(334) 242-4400
Fax: (334) 242-4639

State Archives:
624 Washington Avenue
Montgomery, AL 36130
(334) 242-4361
www.apls.state.al.us/;
www.asc.edu/archives/agis.html

Unclaimed Property:
PO Box 302520
Montgomery, AL 36132
(334) 242-9614

Veteran Affairs Regional Office:
345 Perry Hill Road
Montgomery, AL 36109

Vital Records:
Center for Health Statistics
PO Box 5625
Montgomery, AL 36103-5625

Marriage: $12 1936-
Divorce: $12 1950-
Birth: $12 1908-
Death: $12 1908-

Office of Child Support
Enforcement:
50 Ripley Street
Montgomery, AL 36130-1801
(334) 242-9300
Fax: (334) 242-0606
(800)-284-4347 *

ALASKA- www.state.ak.us

Department of Motor Vehicles:
Department of Public Safety
Motor Vehicle Division
Attn. Research
5700 East Tudor Road
Anchorage, AK 99507
(907) 465-4335
Fax: (907) 463-5860

Drivers License:
Department of Public Safety
Pouch N
Juneau, AK 99801
(907) 465-4335
Fax: (907) 463-5860

State Archives:
141 Willoughby Avenue
Juneau, AK 99801
(907) 465-2270
www.educ.state.ak.us/lam

Unclaimed Property:
  Department of Revenue
  PO Box 110420
  Juneau, AK 99811-0420
  465-4653
  www.revenue.state.ak.us/iea/
  ieunprop.htm

Vital Records:
  Department of Health &
  Social Services
  PO Box 110675
  Juneau, AK 99811-0675
  (907) 465-3038
  Fax: (907) 465-3618
  health.hss.state.ak.us/htmlstuf/
  dph/vitals/vitalst.htm

Office of Child Support
Enforcement:
  550 W Seventh Avenue,
  Suite 310
  Anchorage, AK 99501-6699
  (907) 269-6900
  Fax: (907) 269-6813
  (800)-478-3300 *

ARIZONA-www.state.az.us

Department of Motor Vehicles:
  Motor Vehicle Division
  Title Records
  1801 W Jefferson Avenue
  Phoenix, AZ 85007
  (602) 255-8359

Drivers License:
  Motor Vehicle Division
  1801 W Jefferson Street
  Phoenix, AZ 85007
  (602) 255-8359

State Archives:
  1700 W Washington
  Room 200
  Phoenix, AZ 85007
  (602) 542-4035
  www.dlapr.lib.az.us/
  www.azleg.state.az.us/
  othergvt.htm

Unclaimed Property:
  Department of Revenue
  1600 W Monroe
  Phoenix, AZ 85007
  (602) 542-4643

Veteran Affairs Regional Office:
  3225 N Central Avenue
  Phoenix, AZ 85012

Vital Records:
  Office of Vital Records
  PO Box 3887
  Phoenix, AZ 85030
  (602) 255-2501
  Fax: (602) 249-3040
    Marriage: County
    Divorce: County
    Birth: $6-9 1950-
    Death: $6 1887-

Office of Child Support
Enforcement:
  PO Box 40458
  Phoenix, AZ 85067
  (602) 252-4045

ARKANSAS-www.state.ar.us

Department of Motor Vehicles:
  Office of Motor Vehicles
  PO Box 1272
  Little Rock, AR 72203

Drivers License:
Office of Drivers Services
PO Box 1272
Little Rock, AR 72203

State Archives:
1 Capitol Mall
Little Rock, AR 72201
(501) 682-6900
www.aslplib.ar.us/;
www.state.ar.us/ahc/ahc.html; *or*
www.state.ar.us/html/ark-
library.html

Unclaimed Property:
Auditor of State
1400 W Third Street,
Suite 100
Little Rock, AR 72201-1811
(501) 682-9174
(800) 252-4648
Fax: (501) 682-6005

Veteran Affairs Regional Office:
PO Box 1280, Bldg 65
North Little Rock, AR 72115

Vital Records:
Division of Vital Records
4815 W Markham Street
Little Rock, AR 72205
(501) 661-2637
    Marriage $5 1917-
    Divorce: $5 1923-
    Birth: $5 1914-
    Death: $4 1917-

Office of Child Support
Enforcement:
712 W Third
Little Rock, AR 72201
(501) 682-8398
Fax: (501) 682-6002
(800)-264-2445** (Payments)
(800)-247-4549** (Program)

CALIFORNIA-www.state.ca.us

Department of Motor Vehicles:
Department of Motor Vehicles
PO Box 944247
Sacramento, CA 94244-2470
(916) 657-8098
www.dmv.ca.gov/

Drivers License:
PO Box 944247
Sacramento, CA 94244-2470
(916) 657-8098

State Archives:
1500 Eleventh Street
Sacramento, CA 95814
(916) 653-7715
www.library.ca.gov/

Unclaimed Property:
PO Box 942850
Sacramento, CA 94250-5873
(916) 445-8318
(800)-992-4647 (in CA)
www.sco.ca.gov/

Veteran Affairs Regional Office:
11000 Wilshire Blvd.
Los Angeles, CA 90024

Oakland Federal Bldg
1301 Clay Street
Oakland, CA 94612-5209

2022 Camino Del Rio N
San Diego, CA 92108

Vital Records:
Office of the State
Registrar of Vital Statistics
304 S Street
Sacramento, CA 95814-0241
(916) 445-2684
Fax: (800)-858-5553 (credit
card)

Office of Child Support
Enforcement:
Department of Social Services
PO Box 944245
Sacramento, CA 95244-2450
(916) 654-1532
Fax: (916) 657-3791
(800)-952-5253*

COLORADO-www.state.co.us

Department of Motor Vehicles:
Title Section
140 W Sixth Avenue
Denver, CO 80204

Drivers License:
Traffic Records Section
140 W Sixth Avenue
Room 103
Denver, CO 80204

State Archives:
1313 Sherman Street
Room 1B-20
Denver, CO 80203
(303) 866-2055

Unclaimed Property:
1560 Broadway, Suite 1225
Denver, CO 80202
(303) 894-2443

Veteran Affairs Regional Office:
PO Box 25126
155 Van Gordon Street
Lakewood, CO 80228

Vital Records:
Department of Public Health
& Environment
4300 Cherry Creek Drive S
Denver, CO 80222-1530
(303) 756-4464
Fax: (800)-423-1108
Marriage: County 1900-
Divorce: County
Birth: $15 1900-
Death: $15 1900-

Office of Child Support
Enforcement:
1575 Sherman Street, 2nd
Floor
Denver, CO 80203-1714
(303) 866-5994
Fax: (303) 866-3574

CONNECTICUT-
www.state.ct.us

Department of Motor Vehicles:
Division of Motor Vehicles
60 State Street
Wethersfield, CT 06109-1896
(860) 566-3720

Drivers License:
Department of Motor Vehicles
Record Section
60 State Street
Wethersfield, CT 06209-1896
(860) 566-3720

State Archives:
231 Capitol Avenue
Hartford, CT 06106
(860) 566-4460
www.cslnet.ctstateu.edu/spirit.lib.
uconn.edu/ConnState/Libararies/
CTLibraries.html

Unclaimed Property:
Office of State Treasurer
55 Elm Street
Hartford, CT 06106
702-3050
www.state.ct.us/ott/ucp.htm

Veteran Affairs Regional Office:
450 Main Street
Hartford, CT 06103

Vital Records:
Contact the town in which the
event occurred. Dates of records
will vary from town to town. Flat
fee of $5. Contact the Department
of Public Health only if you need
additional information regarding
the contact for the town in which
the event occurred.
Connecticut Department of
Public Health
Vital Records Unit
150 Washington Street
Hartford, CT 06106
(203) 509-7899

Office of Child Support
Enforcement:
Department of Social Services
25 Sigourney Street
Hartford, CT 06106-5033
(860) 424-5251
Fax: (860) 951-2996
(800)-228-5437** (problems)
(800)-647-8872**
(information)
(800)-698-0572** (payments)

DELAWARE-www.state.de.us

Department of Motor Vehicles:
Attn. Correspondence Pool
PO Box 698
Dover, DE 19903
(302) 739-3147
Fax: (302) 739-2042

Drivers License:
  Department of Public Safety
  Motor Vehicles Division
  PO Box 698
  Dover, DE 19901
  (302) 739-4343
  Fax: (302) 739-2602

State Archives:
  Hall of Records
  Dover, DE 19901
  (302) 739-5318
  www.lib.de.us/

Unclaimed Property:
  Delaware State Escheater
  PO Box 8931
  Wilmington, DE 19899-8931
  (302) 577-3349

Veteran Affairs Regional Office:
  1601 Kirkwood Hwy
  Wilmington, DE 19805

Vital Records.
  Office of Vital Statistics
  PO Box 637
  Dover, DE 19903
  (302) 739-4721
    Marriage: $6 1956-
    Divorce: N/A
    Birth: $6 1924-
    Death: $6 1956-

Office of Child Support
Enforcement:
  Delaware Health and Social
  Services
  1901 North Dupont Hwy
  PO Box 904
  New Castle, DE 19720
  (302) 577-4863, 577-4800
  Fax: (302) 577-4873

DISTRICT OF COLUMBIA-
www.capcityonline.com

Department of Motor Vehicles:
  Bureau of Motor Vehicle
  Services
  301 C Street NW
  Washington, DC 20001
  (202) 727-6761

Drivers License:
  Bureau of Motor Vehicle
  Services
  301 C Street N W
  Washington, DC 20001
  (202) 727-6761

Unclaimed Property:
  Office of the Comptroller
  415 Twelfth Street NW
  Room 408
  Washington, DC 20004
  (202) 727-0063

State Archives:
  1300 Naylor Court NW
  Washington, DC 20001
  (202) 727-2052
  Fax: (202) 707-1389
  lcweb.loc.gov/homepage/lchp.html

Veteran Affairs Regional Office:
  1120 Vermont Avenue NW
  Washington, DC 20421

Vital Records:
Division of Vital Records
800 Ninth Street SW
1st Floor
Washington, DC 20024
(202) 645-5909
Marriage: City
Divorce: City
Birth: $12 1874-
Death: $5 1877-

Office of Child Support
Enforcement:
Department of Human
Services
800 Ninth Street SW, 2nd
Floor
Washington, DC 20024-2485
(202) 645-7500

FLORIDA-www.state.fl.us
Florida Government Information
Locator:
www.dos.state.fl.us/fgils/index.
html

Department of Motor Vehicles:
Division of Motor Vehicles
Neil Kirman Bldg A-126
Tallahassee, FL 32301
(904) 488-5665
Fax: (904) 488-8983

Drivers License:
Department of Highway
Safety
Drivers License Division
PO Box 5775
Tallahassee, FL 32314-5775
(904) 487-2369
sun6.dms.state.fl.us/hsmv/
documents/dlfaqsona.html

State Archives:
R. A. Gray Bldg
Tallahassee, FL 32399
(850) 487-2073
www.dos.state.fl.us/dlis/

Unclaimed Property:
Department of Banking &
Finance
101 East Gaines Street
Tallahassee, FL 32399-0350
(904) 488-0357

Veteran Affairs Regional Office:
PO Box 1437
Saint Petersburg, FL 33731

Vital Statistics:
Florida Department of HRS
Office of Vital Statistics
PO Box 210
Jacksonville, FL 32231-0042
(904) 359-6900
Fax: (904) 359-6993
Marriage: $5 1927-
Divorce: $5 1927-
Birth: $9 1865-
Death: $5 1877-

Office of Child Support
Enforcement:
Department of Revenue
PO Box 8030
Tallahassee, FL 32314-8030
(850) 922-9590
Fax: (850) 488-4401

GEORGIA-www.state.ga.us
Georgia Department of Human
Resources Website:
www.ph.dhr.state.ga.us/vital/
vitalrec.htm

Department of Motor Vehicles:
Motor Vehicle Division
126 Trinity-Washington Bldg
Atlanta, GA 30334

Drivers License:
Department of Public Safety
126 Trinity-Washington Bldg
Atlanta, GA 30334
(404) 657-9300

State Archives:
330 Captiol Avenue SE
Atlanta, GA 30334
(404) 656-2358
www.gpls.public.lib.ga.us/
www.state.ga.us/SOS/Archives/

Unclaimed Property:
Department of Revenue
Property Tax Division
270 Washington Street
Room 404
Atlanta, GA 30334
(404) 656-4244

Veteran Affairs Regional Office:
730 Peachtree Street NE
Atlanta, GA 30365

Vital Records:
Division of Public Health
Vital Records Service
Room 217-H
47 Trinity Avenue SW
Atlanta, GA 30334-5600
(404) 656-4750
Marriage: $10 1952-
Divorce: County
Birth: $10 1919-
Death: $10 1919-

Office of Child Support
Enforcement:
PO Box 38450
Atlanta, GA 30334-0450
(404) 657-3851
Fax: (404) 657-3326
(800)-227-7993*

HAWAII-www.state.hi.us/

Department of Motor Vehicles:
Division of Motor Vehicle
1455 S Beretania Street
Honolulu, HI 96814

Drivers License:
Violations Bureau
824 Bethel
Honolulu, HI 96813

State Archives:
Iolani Palace Grounds
Honolulu, HI 96813
(808) 586-0329

Unclaimed Property:
PO Box 150
Honolulu, HI 96810-0150
(808) 586-1589

Veteran Affairs Regional Office:
PO Box 50188
Honolulu, HI 96850

Vital Records:
Department of Health
Vital Records
PO Box 3378
Honolulu, HI 96801
(808) 586-4539
Marriage: $10 1910-
Divorce: $2 1951-
Birth: $10 1910-

Office of Child Support
Enforcement:
Department of Attorney
General
680 Iwilei Street, Suite 490
Honolulu, HI 96817
(808) 587-3698

IDAHO-www.state.id.us

Department of Motor Vehicles:
Idaho Transportation
Department
Vehicle Research
PO Box 34
Boise, ID 83731-0034
(208) 334-8663
Fax: (208) 334-8658

Drivers License:
Idaho Transportation
Department
Vehicle Research
PO Box 34
Boise, ID 83731-0034
(208) 334-8736
Fax: (208) 334-8739

State Archives
450 N Fourth Street
Boise, ID 83702
(208) 334-3356

Unclaimed Property:
PO Box 36
Boise, ID 83722-2240
(208) 334-7623

Veteran Affairs Regional Office:
805 W Franklin Street
Boise, ID 83702

Vital Records:
Center for Vital Statistics &
Health Policy
450 W State Street
1st Floor
Boise, ID 83720-0036
(208) 334-5976
Fax: (208) 389-9096 (with
credit card charge)
Marriage: $10 1947-
Divorce: $10 1947-
Birth: $10 1911-
Death: $10 1911-

Office of Child Support
Enforcement:
Department of Health and
Welfare
450 W State Street, 5th Floor
Boise, ID 83720-5005
(208) 334-5710
Fax: (208) 334-0666
(800)-356-9868**

ILLINOIS-www.state.il.us

Department of Motor Vehicles:
Secretary of State
Vehicle Records Inquiry
Section
4th Floor, Centennial Bldg
Springfield, IL 62756

Drivers License:
Secretary of State
Drivers Service Section
2701 South Dirksen Parkway
Springfield, IL 62723

State Archives:
Capitol Bldg
Room 213
Springfield, IL 62756
(217) 782-4682
www.sos.state.il.us/depts/library/
isl-home.html
www.library.sos.state.il.us/
internet/spotlite.html

Unclaimed Property:
Department of Financial
Institutions
500 Iles Park Place
Springfield, IL 62718
(217) 785-6995

Veteran Affairs Regional Office:
PO Box 8136
Chicago, IL 60680

Vital Records:
Department of Health
Division of Vital Records
605 W Jefferson
Springfield, IL 62702-5097
(217) 782-6554
Fax: (217) 523-2648 (with
credit card charge)
Marriage & Divorce: $5
1962-(Verification only)
Birth: $15 1916_
Death: $10 1916_ (certified
copy $15)

Office of Child Support
Enforcement:
Department of Public Aid
509 South Sixth
Mariott Bldg
PO Box 19405
Springfield, IL 62701-1825
(217) 524-4602
Fax: (217) 524-4608
(800)-447-4278*

INDIANA-www.state.in.us

Department of Motor Vehicles:
Bureau of Motor Vehicles
Room N404
100 North Senate Avenue
Indianapolis, IN 46204
(317) 233-6000

Drivers License:
Bureau of Motor Vehicles
Drivers Records
Indiana Government Center
North
Room N405
Indianapolis, IN 46204
(317) 232-2894

State Archives
IGCS, 402 W Washington
Street #W472
Indianapolis, IN 46204
(317) 232-3373
www.ai.org/acin/icpr/index.html

Unclaimed Property:
402 W Washington, Suite
C-531
Indianapolis, IN 46204
232-6348
*ideanet.doe.state.in.us/htmls/ag.
html*

Veteran Affairs Regional Office:
575 N Pennsylvania Street
Indianapolis, IN 46204

Vital Records:
Department of Health
PO Box 7125
Indianapolis, IN 46206-7125
(317) 233-1325
(317) 233-2700 (credit card)
Fax: (317) 383-6210 (credit
card)
  Marriage: County
  Divorce: County
  Birth: $6 1907-
  Death: $4 1907-
*www.state.in.us/doh/html/bdcert.
html*

Office of Child Support
Enforcement:
402 W Washington Street
Room W360
Indianapolis, IN 46204
(317) 233-5437
Fax: (317) 233-4925
(800)-622-4932**

IOWA-www.state.ia.us

Department of Motor Vehicles:
Department of Transportation
Office of Vehicle Registration
Lucas State Office Bldg
Des Moines, IA 50319

Drivers License:
Department of Transportation
Office of Driver's Services
Lucas State Office Bldg
Des Moines, IA 50319

State Archives:
402 Iowa Avenue
Iowa City, IA 52240
(515) 281-8837
*www.silo.lib.ia.us/
www.uiowa/edu/~shsi/library/
library.htm*

Unclaimed Property:
Treasurer
State Capitol Bldg
Des Moines, IA 50319
281-5367
*www.state.ia.us/government/
treasurer*

Veteran Affairs Regional Office:
210 Walnut Street
Des Moines, IA 50309

Vital Records:
Department of Health
Vital Statistics
321 E Twelfth
Des Moines, IA 50319
(515) 255-2414
  Marriage: $10 1880-
  Divorce: County
  Birth: $10 1880-
  Death: $10 1880-

Office of Child Support
Enforcement
    Department of Human
    Services
    Hoover Bldg, 5th Floor
    Des Moines, IA 50319
    (515) 281-5580
    Fax: (515) 281-8854

KANSAS-www.state.ks.us

Department of Motor Vehicles:
    Department of Revenue
    Division of Vehicles
    State Office Bldg
    915 Harrison
    Topeka, KS 66626
    (913) 296-3621
    Fax: (913) 296-3852

Drivers License:
    Division of Vehicles
    Driver Control Bureau
    State Office Bldg
    PO Box 12021
    Topeka, KS 66626-2021
    (913) 296-3671

State Archives:
    6425 SW Sixth Street
    Topeka, KS 66615
    (785) 272-8681 x117
    *www.skyways.lib.ks.us/kansas/ksl/
    ksl.html*

Unclaimed Property:
    900 Jackson, Suite 201
    Topeka, KS 66612-1235
    (913) 296-4165
    www.unclaimed.org

Veteran Affairs Regional Office:
    5500 E Kellogg
    Wichita, KS 67218

Vital Records:
    Office of Vital Statistics
    900 SW Jackson
    Room 151
    Topeka, KS 66612-2221
    (Fax: (913) 357-4332 (credit
    card)
        Marriage: $10 1913-
        Divorce: $10 1951-
        Birth: $10 July 1, 1911-
        Death: $10 1911-

Office of Child Support
Enforcement:
    Department of Social &
    Rehabilitation Services
    300 SW Oakley Street,
    Biddle Bldg
    Topeka, KS 66606
    (913) 296-3237
    Fax: (913) 296-5206
    (800)-432-0152
    (Withholding)
    (800)-570-6743 (Collections)
    (800)-432-3913 (Fraud
    Hotline)

KENTUCKY-www.state.ky.us

Department of Motor Vehicles:
    Department of Vehicle
    Registration
    Motor Vehicle Licensing,
    3rd Floor
    New State Office Bldg
    Frankfort, KY 40622
    (502) 564-4076

Drivers License:
  Division of Driver Licenses
  State Office Bldg
  501 High Street, 2nd Floor
  Frankfort, KY 40622
  (502) 564-6800

State Archives:
  300 Coffee Tree Road
  Frankfort, KY 40602
  (502) 564-8300
  www.kdla.state.ky.us/
  www.kdla.state.ky.us/arch/arch.
  html

Unclaimed Property: Branch
  Kentucky State Treasury
  Department
  Suite 183, Capitol Annex
  Frankfort, KY 40601
  564-4722
  www.unclaimed.org

Veteran Affairs Regional Office:
  545 S Third Street
  Louisville, KY 40202

Vital Records:
  Vital Statistics
  275 E Main Street
  Frankfort, KY 40621
  (502) 564-4212
    Marriage: $6 1958-
    Divorce: $6 1958-
    Birth: $9 1911-
    Death: $6 1911-
  www.kdla.state.ky.us/arch/
  vitalstat.htm

Office of Child Support
Enforcement:
  Cabinet for Families and
  Children
  PO Box 2150
  Frankfort, KY 40602
  (502) 564-2285
  Fax: (502) 564-5988

LOUISIANA-www.state.la.us

Department of Motor Vehicles:
  Office of Motor Vehicles
  Department of Public Safety
  PO Box 64886
  Baton Rouge, LA 70896
  (504) 925-6146

Drivers License:
  Department of Public Safety
  Office of Motor Vehicles
  PO Box 64886
  Baton Rouge, LA 70896
  (504) 925-6009

State Archives:
  3851 Essen Lane
  Baton Rouge, LA 70808
  (504) 922-1000
  smt.state.lib.la.us/

Unclaimed Property:
  Louisiana Department of
  Revenue &Taxation
  PO Box 91010
  Baton Rouge, LA 70821-
  9010
  (504) 925-7407
  Fax: (504) 925-3853
  www.unclaimed.org
  www.rev.state.la.us/dirserv.htm

Veteran Affairs Regional Office:
  701 Loyola Avenue
  New Orleans, LA 70113

Vital Records:
  Vital Records Registry
  PO Box 60630
  New Orleans, LA 70160
  (504) 568-5150 /
  (504) 568-5152 /
  (504) 568-8353
  Fax: (504) 568-5391 (credit
  card)
      Marriage: Parish ($5 last 50
      years)
      Divorce: N/A (except for
      Orleans Parish)
      Birth: $15 last 100 years
      Death: $5 last 50 years

Office of Child Support
Enforcement:
  PO Box 94065
  Baton Rouge, LA 70804-
  4065
  (504) 342-4780
  Fax: (504) 342-7397
  (800)-256-4650* (Payments)

MAINE-www.state.me.us

Department of Motor Vehicles:
  Department of State
  Motor Vehicle Division
  29 State House Station
  Augusta, ME 04333-0029
  (207) 287-3556
  Fax: (207) 287-5219

Drivers License:
  Department of State
  Motor Vehicle Division
  29 State House Station
  Augusta, ME 04333
  (207) 287-9005
  Fax: (207) 287-2592
  www.state.me.us/sos/bmv/dlc/
  dlchmpg.htm

State Archives:
  84 State House Station
  Augusta, ME 04333
  (207) 287-5793
  Fax: (207) 287-5624
  www.state.me.us/msl/mslhome.
  htm
  www.state.me.us/sos/arc/general/
  admin/mawww001.htm

Unclaimed Property:
  Treasury Department
  39 State House Station
  Augusta, ME 04333-0039
  (207) 287-6668

Veteran Affairs Regional Office:
  Togus, ME 04330

Vital Records:
  Division of Vital Records
  221 State Street, Station 11
  Augusta, ME 04333-0011
  (207) 287-3181
  Fax: (207) 287-1907 (credit
  card)
      Marriage: $10 1923-
      Divorce: $10 1923-
      Birth: $10 1923-
      Death: $10 1923-

Office of Child Support
Enforcement:
  Bureau of Family
  Independence
  State House Station
  11 Whitten Road
  Augusta, ME 04333
  (207) 287-2886
  Fax: (207) 287-5096
  (800)-371-3101*

MARYLAND-
www.mec.state.md.us

Department of Motor Vehicles:
  Motor Vehicle
  Administration
  6601 Ritchie Highway NE
  Glen Burnie, MD 21062

Drivers License:
  Motor Vehicle
  Administration
  6601 Ritchie Highway NE
  Glen Burnie, MD 21062

State Archives:
  350 Rowe Blvd.
  Annapolis, MD 21401
  (410) 974-3915
  Fax: (410) 974-3895
  www.mdarchives.state.md.us

Unclaimed Property:
  301 W Preston Street
  Baltimore, MD 21201-2385
  225-1700
  sailor.lib.md.us/md/comptroller/
  money.html

Veteran Affairs Regional Office:
  31 Hopkins Plaza
  Baltimore, MD 21201

Vital Records:
  Division of Vital Records
  4201 Patterson Avenue
  Baltimore, MD 21215
  (410) 764-3028
  Fax: (410) 358-0781 (credit
  card)
    Marriage: $4 1951-
    Divorce: Verification only
    1962-
    Birth: $4 1875-
    Death: $4 1969-
  www.mdarchives.state.md.us/msa/
  refserv/html/vitalrec.html

Office of Child Support
Enforcement:
  Department of Human
  Resources
  311 W Saratoga Street
  Baltimore, MD 21201
  (410) 767-7619
  Fax: (410) 333-8992
  (800)-332-6347*

MASSACHUSETTS-
www.state.ma.us

Department of Motor Vehicles:
  Registrar of Motor Vehicles
  1135 Tremont Street
  Boston, MA 02120
  (617) 351-9806

Drivers License:
  Registry of Motor Vehicles
  1135 Tremont Street
  Boston, MA 02120
  (617) 351-9834

State Archives:
  State House
  Room 337
  Boston, MA 02133
  (617) 727-9150
  Fax: (617) 742-4722
  www.mlin.lib.ma.us/

Unclaimed Property:
  1 Ashburton Place, 12th Floor
  Boston, MA 02108
  (617) 367-0400

Veteran Affairs Regional Office:
  John F. Kennedy Federal Bldg
  Boston, MA 02203

Vital Records:
  Registry of Vital Statistics
  470 Atlantic Avenue
  2nd Floor
  Boston, MA 02210
  (617) 753-8600
    Marriage: $11 1901-
    Divorce: Through probate
    courts
    Birth: $11 1901-
    Death: $11 1901-

Office of Child Support
Enforcement:
  Department of Revenue
  141 Portland Street
  Cambridge, MA 02139-1937
  Fax: (617) 621-4991
  (800)-332-2733**

MICHIGAN-
www.migov.stat.mi.us

Department of Motor Vehicles:
  Department of State Bureau of
  Driver & Vehicle Services
  7064 Crowner Drive
  Lansing, MI 48918
  (517) 322-1624
  Fax: (517) 322-1181

Drivers License:
  Department of State Bureau of
  Driver & Vehicle Services
  7064 Crowner Drive
  Lansing, MI 49818
  (517) 322-1624
  Fax: (517) 322-1181

State Archives:
  717 W Allegan
  Lansing, MI 48918
  (517) 373-1408
  Fax: (517) 373-0851
  www.sos.state.mi.us/history/
  archive/archive.html

Unclaimed Property:
  Department of Treasury
  Lansing, MI 48922
  335-4327
  www.unclaimed.org

Veteran Affairs Regional Office:
  477 Michigan Avenue
  Detroit, MI 48226

Vital Records:
Department of Health
3423 N Martin Luther King
Blvd
PO Box 30195
Lansing, MI 48909
(517) 335-8656
Fax: (517) 335-8666
    Marriage: $13 1897-
    Divorce: $13 1867-
    Birth: $13 1867-
    Death: $13 1867-
www.sos.state.mi.us/history/
archive/circular/c19.html

Office of Child Support
Enforcement:
Department of Social Services
PO Box 30478
Lansing, MI 48909-7978

Street Address:
7109 W Saginaw Hwy
Lansing, MI 48909-7978
(517) 373-7570
Fax: (517) 373-4980

MINNESOTA-www.state.mn.us

Department of Motor Vehicles:
Department of Public Safety
Driver and Vehicle Services
Division
395 John Ireland Blvd
Room 107
Saint Paul, MN 55155
(612) 296-6911
www.dps.state.mn.us/dvshome.
html

Drivers License:
Department of Public Safety
Drivers License
395 John Ireland Blvd
Room 107
Saint Paul, MN 55155
(612) 296-6911
www.dps.state.mn.us/dvshome.
html

State Archives:
345 Kellogg Blvd., W
Saint Paul, MN 55102
(651) 296-2143

Unclaimed Property:
Minnesota Commerce
Department
133 East Seventh Street
Saint Paul, MN 55101
(612) 296-2568

Veteran Affairs Regional Office:
Bishop Henry Whipple
Federal Bldg
Fort Snelling, MN 55111

Vital Records:
Department of Health
717 Delaware Street SE
Minneapolis, MN 55414
(612) 623-5121
Fax: (612) 331-5776 (credit
card)
    Marriage: County
    Divorce: County
    Birth: $14 1900-
    Death: $11 1908-

Office of Child Support
Enforcement:
    Department of Human
    Services
    444 Lafayette Road, 4th Floor
    Saint Paul, MN 55155-3846
    (612) 215-1714
    Fax: (612) 297-4450

MISSISSIPPI-www.state.ms.us

Department of Motor Vehicles:
    State Tax Commission
    Department of Motor Vehicles
    Title Division
    PO Box 1140
    Jackson, MS 39205

Drivers License:
    Mississippi Highway Safety
    Patrol
    Drivers License Division
    PO Box 958
    Jackson, MS 39205

State Archives:
    PO Box 571
    Jackson, MS 39205
    (601) 359-6850
    www.mlc.lib.ms.us/
    www.mlc.lib.ms.us/deposit.
    htm#govdoc

Unclaimed Property:
    PO Box 138
    Jackson, MS 39205-0138
    359-3600
    www.unclaimed.org

Veteran Affairs Regional Office:
    100 W Capitol Street
    Jackson, MS 39269

Vital Records:
    Division of Vital Records
    PO Box 1700
    Jackson, MS 39215
    (601) 960-7981
    Fax: (601) 354-6174 (credit
    card)
        Marriage: $10 1926-
        Divorce: County
        Birth: $12 1912-
        Death: $10 1912-

Office of Child Support
Enforcement:
    Department of Human
    Services
    PO Box 352
    Jackson, MS 39205
    (601) 359-4861
    Fax: (601) 359-4415
    (800)-434-5437**(Jackson)
    (800)-354-6039 (Hines,
    Rankin, and Madison
    Counties)

MISSOURI-www.state.mo.us/

Department of Motor Vehicles:
    Motor Vehicle Bureau
    PO Box 100
    Jefferson City, MO 65701
    (573) 751-4300
    Fax: (573) 526-4769

Drivers License:
  Bureau of Driver Licenses
  PO Box 200
  Department of Revenue
  Jefferson City, MO 65101-
  0200
  (573) 751-4391
  Fax: (573) 526-4769

State Archives:
  PO Box 778
  Jefferson City, MO 65102
  (573) 751-6500
  Fax (573) 526-7333
  www.mosl.sos.state.mo.us/

Unclaimed Property:
  PO Box 1272
  Jefferson City, MO 65102-
  1272
  751-0840
  www.unclaimed.org

Veteran Affairs Regional Office:
  400 S Eighteenth Street
  Saint Louis, MO 63125

Vital Records:
  Department of Health
  Bureau of Vital Records
  PO Box 570
  Jefferson City, MO 65102
  (573) 751-6387
    Marriage: $10 July 1948-
    Divorce: $10 July 1948-
    Birth: $10 1910-
    Death: $10 1910-

Office of Child Support
Enforcement:
  PO Box 2320
  Jefferson City, MO 65102-
  2320
  (573) 751-4301
  Fax: (573) 751-8450
  (800)-859-7999**

MONTANA-www.mt.gov

Department of Motor Vehicles:
  Registrar's Bureau
  925 Main Street
  Deer Lodge, MT 58722

Drivers License:
  Montana Highway Patrol
  303 N Roberts
  Helena, MT 59620

State Archives:
  225 North Roberts Street
  Helena, MT 59620
  (406) 444-4775
  msl.mt.gov/

Veterans Affairs Regional
Office:
  Fort Harrison, MT 59636

Unclaimed Property:
  Department of Revenue
  Mitchell Bldg
  Helena, MT 59620
  (406) 444-2425

Vital Records:
  Department of Health and
  Human Services
  111 N Sanders #215
  Helena, MT 59620
  (406) 444-4228
    Marriage: County 1943-
    Divorce: County 1943-
    Birth: $10 1907-
    Death: $10 1907-

Office of Child Support
Enforcement:
  Department of Health and
  Human Services
  PO Box 202943
  Helena, MT 59620
  (406) 442-7278
  (800)-346-5437*

NEBRASKA-www.state.ne.us/

Department of Motor Vehicles
  PO Box 94789
  Lincoln, NE 68509-4789
  (402) 471-4343
  (800) 747-8177

Drivers License:
  Department of Motor Vehicles
  Driver Records Section
  PO Box 94789
  Lincoln, NE 68509-4789
  (402) 471-4343
  (800) 747-8177

State Archives:
  PO Box 82554
  Lincoln, NE 68501
  (402) 471-4785

Unclaimed Property:
  PO Box 94788
  Lincoln, NE 68509
  (402) 471-2455

Veteran Affairs Regional Office:
  5631 S Forty-eighth Street
  Lincoln, NE 68516

Vital Records:
  Department of Health
  Health Records Management
  Vital Records Unit
  PO Box 95065
  Lincoln, NE 68509-5065
  (402) 471-2871
    Marriage: $9 1909-
    Divorce: $9 1909-
    Birth: $10 1904-
    Death: $9 1904-

Office of Child Support
Enforcement:
  Department of Social Services
  PO Box 95044
  Lincoln, NE 68509
  (402) 471-9160
  Fax: (402) 471-9455
  (800)-831-4573*

NEVADA-www.state.nv.us

Department of Motor Vehicles:
  Registration Division
  Carson City, NV 89711

Drivers License:
  Department of Motor Vehicles
  Drivers License Division
  Carson City, NV 89711

State Archives:
  100 North Stewart
  Carson City, NV 89701
  (702) 687-8317
  Fax: (702) 687-8311
  www.clan.lib.nv.us/docs/nsla.htm

Unclaimed Property:
  2501 East Sahara Avenue
  Suite 304
  Las Vegas, NV 89104
  (702) 486-4140

Veteran Affairs Regional Office:
  1201 Terminal Way
  Reno, NV 89520

Vital Records:
  Office of Vital Statistics
  505 East King Street
  Carson City, NV 89710
    Marriage: County
    Divorce: County
    Birth: $11 1911-
    Death: $8 1911-

Office of Child Support
Enforcement:
  Nevada State Welfare
  Division
  2527 North Carson Street
  Carson City, NV 89706-0113
  (702) 687-4744
  Fax: (702) 684-8026
  (800)-992-0900*

NEW HAMPSHIRE-
www.state.nh.us

Department of Motor Vehicles:
  Department of Safety
  Division of Motor Vehicles
  J. H. Hayes Bldg
  Concord, NH 03305

Drivers License:
  Division of Motor Vehicles
  Drivers License Division
  J. H. Hayes Bldg
  Concord, NH 03305

State Archives:
  107 North Main Street
  Room 204
  Concord, NH 03301
  (603) 271-2236
  Fax: (603) 271-2205
  www.state.nh.us/state/archives.
  htm

Unclaimed Property:
  Treasury Department
  25 Capitol Street
  Room 205
  Concord, NH 03301
  (603) 271-2649

Vital Records:
  Bureau of Vital Records &
  Health Statistics
  Division of Public Health
  Health & Welfare Bldg
  6 Hazen Drive
  Concord, NH 03301-6527
  (603) 271-4650
    Marriage: $10 1640-
    Divorce: $10 1640-
    Birth: $10 1640-
    Death: $10 1640-

Office of Child Support
Enforcement:
  Division of Human Services
  Health and Human Services
  Bldg
  6 Hazen Drive
  Concord, NH 03301-6531
  (603) 271-4427
  Fax: (603) 271-4787
  (800)-852-3345* x4427

NEW JERSEY-www.state.nj.us

Department of Motor Vehicles:
  Bureau of Office Services
  Certified Information Unit
  CN146
  25 South Montgomery Street
  Trenton, NJ 08666
  (609) 292-6500

Drivers License:
  Department of Law and Public
  Safety
  Drivers License Division
  CN142
  West Trenton, NJ 08666
  (609) 292-6500

State Archives:
  2300 Stuyvesant Avenue
  Trenton, NJ 08625
  (609) 530-3203
  Fax: (609) 396-2454

*www.state.nj.us/statelibrary/njlib.
htm*

Unclaimed Property:
  Department of the Treasury
  Property Administration
  CN 214
  Trenton, NJ 08646
  (609) 984-8234

Veteran Affairs Regional Office:
  20 Washington Place
  Newark, NJ 07102

Vital Records:
  Bureau of Vital Statistics
  CN 370
  Room 504
  Trenton, NJ 08625
  (609) 292-4087
  (609) 633-2860 (Vital check-
  $5)
  Fax: (609) 392-4292
    Marriage: $4 1878-
    Divorce: N/A
    Birth: $4 1878-
    Death: $4 1878-

Office of Child Support
Enforcement:
  Division of Family
  Development
  Department of Human
  Services
  PO Box 716
  Trenton, NJ 08625-0716
  (609) 588-2915
  Fax: (609) 588-3369
  (800)-621-5437**

NEW MEXICO-
www.state.nm.us

Department of Motor Vehicles:
Motor Vehicles Division
PO Box 1028
Santa Fe, NM 87504-1028
(505) 827-2290

Drivers License:
Motor Vehicle Division
Driver Services Bureau
PO Box 1028
Santa Fe, NM 87504
(505) 827-2234

State Archives:
404 Montezuma
Santa Fe, NM 87503
(505) 827-7332
Fax: (505) 827-7331

Unclaimed Property:
Special Tax Programs &
Services
PO Box 25123
Santa Fe, NM 87504-5123
(505) 827-0767
827-0769
www.unclaimed.org

Vital Records:
Bureau of Vital Records &
Health Statistics
1190 Street Francis Drive
PO Box 26110
Sante Fe, NM 87502
(505) 827-0121
(505) 827-2316 (credit card)
Fax: (505) 984-1048
Marriage: County
Divorce: County
Birth: $10 1919- (a few
available prior to 1919)
Death: $5 1919- (a few
available prior to 1919)

Office of Child Support
Enforcement:
Department of Human
Services
PO Box 25109
Santa Fe, NM 87504

Street Address:
2025 S Pacheco
Santa Fe, NM 87504
(505) 827-7200
Fax: (505) 827-7285
(800)-432-6217*

NEW YORK-www.state.ny.us

Department of Motor Vehicles:
Empire State Plaza
Swan Street Bldg
Room 430
Albany, NY 12228
(518) 474-4572

Drivers License:
  Department of Motor Vehicles
  Empire State Plaza
  Swan Street Bldg
  Room 420
  Albany, NY 12228
  (518) 474-2381

State Archives:
  33 Cultural Education Center
  Room 10A
  Albany, NY 12230
  (518) 473-7091
  Fax: (518) 473-9985
  www.unix2.nysed.gov/
  www.sara.nysed.gov

Unclaimed Property:
  Alfred E Smith Bldg
  9th Floor
  Albany, NY 12236
  (518) 474-4038

Veteran Affairs Regional Office:
  111 W Huron Street
  Buffalo, NY 14202
  245 W Houston Street
  New York, NY 10014

Vital Records:
  Department of Health
  Empire State Plaza
  Albany, NY 12237-0023
  (518) 474-3055
  Fax: (518) 474-3077
    Marriage: $5 1880-
    Divorce: $15 1880-
    Birth: $15 1880-
    Death: $15 1880-
    (Payment by money order
    only)
  www.health.state.ny.us

New York City
Bureau of Vital Records
125 Worth Street
New York, NY 10013
(212) 669-8898

Office of Child Support
Enforcement:
  Department of Social Services
  PO Box 14
  One Commerce Plaza
  Albany, NY 12260-0014
  (518) 474-9081
  Fax: (518) 486-3127
  (800)-343-8859*

NORTH CAROLINA-
www.state.nc.us

Department of Motor Vehicles:
  Vehicle Registration
  Division of Motor Vehicles
  1100 New Bern Avenue
  Raleigh, NC 27697
  (919) 715-7000

Drivers License:
  Traffic Records Section
  Division of Motor Vehicles
  1100 New Bern Avenue
  Raleigh, NC 27697
  (919) 715-7000

State Archives:
  109 E Jones Street
  Raleigh, NC 27601
  (919) 733-7305
  Fax: (919) 733-1354
  statelibrary.dcr.state.nc.us/
  ncslhome.htm
  www.ah.dcr.state.nc.us

Unclaimed Property:
   325 North Salisbury Street
   Raleigh, NC 27603-1385
   (919) 733-6876
   www.unclaimed.org
   www.treasurer.state.nc.us/
   Treasurer/escheat.htm

Veteran Affairs Regional Office:
   251 N Main Street
   Winston-Salem, NC 27155

Vital Records:
   Division of Vital Records
   PO Box 29537
   Raleigh, NC 27626
   (919) 733-3000
      Marriage: $10 1962-
      Divorce: $10 1958-
      Birth: $10 1913-
      Death: $10 1930-

Office of Child Support
Enforcement:
   Department of Human
   Resources
   Division of Social Services
   100 East Six Forks Road
   Raleigh, NC 27609-7750
   (919) 571-4114
   Fax: (919) 881-2280
   (800)-992-9457*

NORTH DAKOTA-
www.state.nd.us

Department of Motor Vehicles:
   Capitol Grounds
   Bismarck, ND 58505

Drivers License:
   Capitol Grounds
   Bismarck, ND 58505

State Archives:
   612 E Boulevard Avenue
   Bismarck, ND 58505
   (701) 328-2668
   www.ndsl.lib.state.nd.us/hist/

Unclaimed Property:
   State Land Department
   PO Box 5523
   Bismarck, ND 58506-5523
   (701) 328-2805

Vital Records:
   Division of Vital Records
   State Capitol
   600 E Boulevard Avenue
   Bismarck, ND 58505-0200
   (701) 328-2360
      Marriage: $5 July 1925-
      Divorce: County
      Birth: $7 1870-
      Death: $5 1881-
   www.health.state.nd.us/

Office of Child Support
Enforcement:
   Department of Human
   Services
   PO Box 7190
   Bismarck, ND 58507-7190
   (701) 328-3582
   Fax: (701) 328-5497
   (800)-755-8530*

OHIO-www.state.oh.us

Department of Motor Vehicles:
Department of Highway
Safety
Bureau of Motor Vehicles
7300 Kimberly Pkwy.
Columbus, OH 43232
(614) 752-7671

Drivers License:
Bureau of Motor Vehicles
4300 Kimberly Pkwy.
Columbus, OH 43232
(614) 752-7600

State Archives:
Seventeenth Avenue &
Interstate 71
Columbus, OH 43211
(614) 297-2300
Fax: (614) 297-2411
winslo.ohio.gov/ohswww/statearc.
html

Unclaimed Property:
77 South High Street
Columbus, OH 43266-0545
466-4433
www.unclaimed.org

Veteran Affairs Regional Office:
1240 E Ninth Street
Cleveland, OH 44199

Vital Records:
Department of Health
Vital Statistics
PO Box 15098
Columbus, OH 43215-0098
(614) 466-2531
Marriage: County
Divorce: County
Birth: $7 1908-
Death: $7 1945-

Office of Child Support
Enforcement:
Department of Human
Services
30 East Broad Street,
31st Floor
Columbus, OH 43266-0423
(614) 752-6561
Fax: (614) 752-9760
(800) 686-1556

OKLAHOMA-www.state.ok.us

Department of Motor Vehicles:
Motor Vehicle Division
2501 Lincoln Blvd.
Oklahoma City, OK 73194

Drivers License:
Department of Public Safety
PO Box 11415
Oklahoma City, OK 73136

State Archives:
200 NE Eighteenth Street
Oklahoma City, OK 73105-
3298
(405) 521-2502
Fax: (405) 525-7804
www.state.ok.us/~odl/

Unclaimed Property:
Oklahoma Tax Commission
2501 Lincoln Boulevard
Oklahoma City, OK 73194-
0010
521-4275
www.unclaimed.org

Veteran Affairs Regional Office:
125 S Main Street
Muskogee, OK 74401

Vital Records:
Health Department
Division of Vital Records
1000 NE Tenth Street
Oklahoma City, OK 73152
(405) 271-4040
Marriage: County
Divorce: County
Birth: $5 1908-
Death: $10 1908-

Office of Child Support
Enforcement:
Department of Human
Services
PO Box 53552
Oklahoma City, OK 73152

Street Address:
2409 N Kelley Avenue
Annex Bldg
Oklahoma City, OK 73111
(405) 522-5871
Fax: (405) 522-2753
(800)-522-2922**

OREGON-www.state.or.us/

Department of Motor Vehicles:
Motor Vehicle Division
1905 Lona Avenue NE
Salem, OR 97314

Drivers License:
Motor Vehicle Division
1905 Lona Avenue NE
Salem, OR 97314

State Archives:
800 Summer Street NE
Salem, OR 97310
(503) 373-0701
Fax: (503) 373-0953
www.osl.state.or.us/oslhome.html

Unclaimed Property:
775 Summer Street NE
Salem, OR 97310
(503) 378-3805 ext.450

Veteran Affairs Regional Office:
1220 SW Third Avenue
Portland, OR 97207

Vital Records:
Health Division
Vital Records
PO Box 14050
Portland, OR 97293
(503) 731-4108
(503) 234-8417 (credit card)
Marriage: $15 1906-
Divorce: $15 1925-
Birth: $15 1903-
Death: $15 1903-
*www.ohd.hr.state.or.us/cdpe/chs/
certif/certfaqs.htm*

Office of Child Support
Enforcement:
Adult and Family Services
Division
Department of Human
Resources
260 Liberty Street NE
Salem, OR 97310
(503) 378-5567
Fax: (503) 391-5526
(800)-850-0228*
(800)-850-0294 (Rotary)

PENNSYLVANIA-
www.state.pa.us

Department of Motor Vehicles:
Bureau of Motor Vehicles
Transportation & Safety Bldg
Harrisburg, PA 17122

Drivers License:
Department of Transportation
Bureau of Drivers Licensing
Room 212
Transportation & Safety Bldg
Harrisburg, PA 17120

State Archives:
PO Box 1026
Harrisburg, PA 17108-1026
(717) 783-9872
Fax: (717) 787-4822
www.state.pa.us/PAExec/
Historical Museum/DARMS/
overview.htm

Unclaimed Property:
Pennsylvania State Treasury
PO Box 1837
Harrisburg, PA 17105-1837
(800) 222-2046 (Claims
inquiries)
(800) 379-3999 (Reporting
questions and Instructions)
www.unclaimed.org

Veteran Affairs Regional Office:
5000 Wissahickon Avenue
Philadelphia, PA 19101

Vital Records:
Division of Vital Records
PO Box 1528
New Castle, PA 16103
(412) 656-3100 (before 4:00
p.m. EDT)
Fax: (412) 652-8951 (credit
card)
Marriage: County
Divorce: County
Birth: $4 1906-
Death: $3 1906-

Office of Child Support
Enforcement:
Department of Public Welfare
PO Box 8018
Harrisburg, PA 17105
(717) 787-3672
Fax: (717) 787-9706
(800)-932-0211**

RHODE ISLAND-
www.state.ri.us

Department of Motor Vehicles:
Registrar of Motor Vehicles
State Office Bldg
Providence, RI 02903

Drivers License:
Registry of Motor Vehicles
Room 101 G
State Office Bldg
Providence, RI 02903

State Archives:
State House
Room 220
Providence, RI 02903
(401) 222-2353
Fax: (401) 277-3199
www.dsls.state.ri.us/

Unclaimed Property:
PO Box 1435
Providence, RI 02901-1435
(401) 277-6505
*www.state.ri.us/treas/money1st.
htm*

Veteran Affairs Regional Office:
380 Westminster Mall
Providence, RI 02903

Vital Records:
Department of Health
3 Capitol Hill
Room 101
Providence, RI 02908-5097
(401) 277-2812
Marriage: $15 1894-
Divorce: County
Birth: $15 1894-
Death: $15 1944-

Office of Child Support
Enforcement:
Division of Administration
and Taxation
77 Dorrance Street
Providence, RI 02903
(401) 277-2847
Fax: (401) 277-6674
(800)-638-5437*

SOUTH CAROLINA-
www.state.sc.us

Department of Motor Vehicles:
Motor Vehicle Division
Department. of Highway &
Public Transportation
Columbia, SC 29216

Drivers License:
Department of Highways and
Public Transportation
Drivers Records Clerk,
Section 201
PO Box 100178
Columbia, SC 29202-3178
(803) 737-2940

State Archives:
8301 Park Lane Road
Columbia, SC 29223
(605) 896-6100
Fax: (803) 734-8820
www.state.sc.us/scsl/
www.state.sc.us/scdah

Unclaimed Property:
State Treasurers Office
PO Box 11778
Columbia, SC 29211-1778
(803) 734-2629
www.unclaimed.org

Veteran Affairs Regional Office:
 1801 Assembly Street
 Columbia, SC 29201

Vital Records:
 Division of Vital Records
 2600 Bull Street
 Columbia, SC 29201
 (803) 734-4810
 734-6663 (credit card)

Office of Child Support
Enforcement:
 PO Box 1469
 Columbia, SC 29202-1469
 (803) 737-5875
 Fax: (803) 737-6032
 (800)-768-5858**
 (800)-768-6779* (Payments)

**SOUTH DAKOTA-
www.state.sd.us**

Department of Motor Vehicles:
 Department of Revenue
 118 West Capitol
 Pierre, SD 57501
 (605) 773-6883
 Fax: (605) 773-6631

Drivers License:
 Department of Commerce and
 Regulation
 118 West Capitol
 Pierre, SD 57501
 (605) 773-6883
 Fax: (605) 773-6631

State Archives:
 900 Governors Drive
 Pierre, SD 57501-2217
 (605) 741-7996
 Fax: (605) 773-6041
 *www.state.sd.us/state/executive/
 deca/cultural/archives.htm*

Unclaimed Property:
 500 East Capitol Avenue
 Pierre, SD 57501
 (605) 773-3378
 *www.state.sd.us/state/executive/
 treasurer/prop.htm*

Vital Records:
 Department of Health
 c/o Vital Statistics
 600 E Capitol Avenue
 Pierre, SD 57501-3185
 (605) 773-4961
  Marriage: $7 1905-
  Divorce: $7 1905-
  Birth: $7 1905-
  Death: $7 1905-

Office of Child Support
Enforcement:
 Department of Social Services
 700 Governor's Drive
 Pierre, SD 57501-2291
 (605) 773-3641
 Fax: (605) 773-5246

TENNESSEE-www.state.tn

Department of Motor Vehicles:
 Motor Vehicle Division
 44 Vantage Way
 Nashville, TN 37228

Drivers License:
  Department of Safety
  1150 Foster Avenue
  Nashville, TN 37249

State Archives:
  403 Seventh Avenue N
  Nashville, TN 37243-0312
  (615) 741-7996
  Fax: (615) 741-6471
  www.state.tn.us/sos/statelib/
  tslahome.htm
  www.magibox.net/~tfc/assoc/
  states/tn.htm

Unclaimed Property:
  Andrew Jackson Bldg
  9th Floor
  Nashville, TN 37243-0242
  (615) 741-6499

Veteran Affairs Regional Office:
  110 Ninth Avenue S
  Nashville, TN 37203

Vital Records:
  Division of Vital Records
  3rd Floor
  Tennessee Towers Bldg
  Nashville, TN 37247-0350
  741-1763
  (615) 741-0778 (with credit
  card charge)
  Fax: (615) 726-2559
    Marriage: $10 July 1, 1945-
    Divorce: $10 July 1, 1945-
    Birth: $10 1914-
    Death: $5 1914-
  www.state.tn.us/health/vr/index.
  html

Office of Child Support
Enforcement:
  Department of Human
  Services
  Citizens Plaza Bldg
  12th Floor
  400 Deadrick Street
  Nashville, TN 37248-7400
  (615) 313-4880
  Fax: (615) 532-2791
  (800)-838-6911* (Payments)

TEXAS-www.state.tx.us

Department of Motor Vehicles:
  Motor Vehicle Division
  Department of Highway &
  Public Transportation
  Fortieth & Jackson Avenue
  Austin, TX 78779
  (512) 465-7611
  Fax: (512) 465-7736

Drivers License:
  Driver Records Division
  Fortieth & Jackson Avenue
  Austin, TX 78779
  (512) 465-7611
  Fax: (512) 465-7736

State Archives:
  PO Box 12927
  Austin, TX 78711
  (512) 463-5480
  Fax: (512) 463-5436
  www.tsl.state.tx.us/

Unclaimed Property:
  Comptroller of Public
  Accounts
  PO Box 12019
  Austin, TX 78711-2019
  Phone: (512) 463-3120
  Fax: (512) 936-6224
  www.unclaimed.org

Veteran Affairs Regional Office:
  6900 Almeda Road
  Houston, TX 77030
  1400 N Valley Mills Dr.
  Waco, TX 76799

Vital Records:
  Department of Health
  Vital Records
  PO Box 12040
  Austin, TX 78711-2040
  (512) 458-7111 Ext. 3184
  Fax: (512) 458-7711 (credit
  card)
    Marriage: County
    Divorce: County
    Birth: $11 1903-
    Death: $9 1903-

Office of Child Support
Enforcement:
  PO Box 12017
  Austin, TX 78711-2017
  (512) 460-6000
  Fax: (512) 479-6478
  (800) 252-8014**

UTAH-www.state.ut.us

Department of Motor Vehicles:
  State Tax Commission
  Motor Vehicle Division
  State Fair Grounds
  1905 Motor Avenue
  Salt Lake City, UT 84416

Drivers License:
  Drivers License Division
  314 State Office Bldg
  Salt Lake City, UT 84114

State Archives:
  3120 State Office Bldg
  Salt Lake City, UT 84114
  (801) 538-3012
  Fax: (801) 538-3354
  www.archives.state.ut.us/html/
  Records-&-Archives.htm
  www.state.lib.ut.us/

Unclaimed Property:
  State Treasurer's Office
  341 South Main Street, 5th
  Floor
  Salt Lake City, UT 84111
  (801) 533-4101

Veteran Affairs Regional Office:
  125 S State Street
  Salt Lake City, UT 84147

Vital Records:
  Bureau of Records
  288 North 1460 W
  PO Box 142855
  Salt Lake City, UT 84114-
  2855
  (801) 538-6380
  (credit card-$15 service
  charge)

Office of Child Support
Enforcement:
  PO Box 45011
  Salt Lake City, UT 84145-
  0011
  (801) 536-8500
  Fax: (801) 436-8509
  (800)-257-9156**

VERMONT-www.state.vt.us

Department of Motor Vehicles:
  120 State Street
  Montpelier, VT 05603
  (802) 828-2050
  Fax: (802) 828-2098

Drivers License:
  Department of Motor Vehicles
  120 State Street
  Montpelier, VT 05602
  (802) 828-2050
  Fax: (802) 828-2098

State Archives:
  109 State Street
  Montpelier, VT 05609-1101
  (802) 828-2369
  Fax: (802) 828-2496
dol.state.vt.us/archives.htm

Unclaimed Property:
  133 State Street
  Montepelier, VT 05633-6200
  (802) 828-2301
www.state.vt.us/treasurer/
abanprop.htm

Veteran Affairs Regional Office:
  White River Junction, VT
  05009

Vital Records:
  Department of Health
  Vital Records
  PO Box 70
  Burlington, VT 05402
  (802) 863-7275
    Marriage: $7 1988-
    Divorce: $7 1988-
    Birth: $7 1988-
    Death: $7 1988-
  Prior to 1988:
  General Services Center
  Public Records Division
  U.S. Route 2, Middlesex
  Drawer 33
  Montpelier, VT 05633
  (802) 828-3286
  Fax: (802) 828-3710 (for
  genealogy information only)
    Marriage: $7 1760-
    Divorce: $7 1760-
    Birth: $7 1760-
    Death: $7 1760-

Office of Child Support
Enforcement:
  103 South Main Street
  Waterbury, VT 05671-1901
  Fax: (802) 244-1483
  (800)-786-3214**

VIRGINIA-www.state/va/us

Department of Motor Vehicles:
  Department of Motor Vehicles
  PO Box 27412
  Richmond, VA 23269
  (804) 367-6729

Drivers License:
　Department of Motor Vehicles
　Driver Licensing and
　Information
　PO Box 27412
　Richmond, VA 23269
　(804) 367-6729

State Archives:
　800 E Broad Street
　Richmond, VA 23219-1905
　(804) 692-3800
　leo.vsla.edu/

Unclaimed Property:
　Department of Treasury
　PO Box 2478
　Richmond, VA 23218-2478
　(804) 225-2393

Veteran Affairs Regional Office:
　210 Franklin Road SW
　Roanoke, VA 24011

Vital Records:
　Division of Vital Records
　PO Box 1000
　Richmond, VA 23218-1000
　(804) 644-2537 (check- credit
　card)
　Fax: (804) 644-2550
　　Marriage: $8 1853-
　　Divorce: $8 1853-
　　Birth: $8 1853-
　　Death: $8 1853-

Office of Child Support
Enforcement:
　Department of Social Services
　730 East Broad Street
　Richmond, VA 23219
　(804) 692-1428
　Fax: (804) 692-1405
　(800)-468-8894*

WASHINGTON-www.wa.gov

Department of Motor Vehicles:
　Department of Licensing
　PO Box 9909
　Olympia, WA 98504

Drivers License:
　Department of Licensing
　PO Box 9909
　Olympia, WA 98504

State Archives:
　PO Box 40220
　Olympia, WA 98504-0220
　(360) 586-2660
　Fax: (360) 664-8814
　www.wa.gov/wsl/

Unclaimed Property:
　Department of Revenue
　PO Box 448
　Olympia, WA 98507-0448
　586-2736
　www.wa.gov/DOR/ucp.htm

Veteran Affairs Regional Office:
　915 Second Avenue
　Seattle, WA 98174

Vital Records:
Department of Health
Center for Health Statistics
PO Box 9709
Olympia, WA 98507-9709
(360) 753-5936
753-4379 (fee for credit card)
Fax: (360) 352-2586
　Marriage: $13 1968-
　Divorce: $13 1968-
　Birth: $13 1907-
　Death: $13 1907-

Office of Child Support
Enforcement:
Department of Social Health
Services
PO Box 9162
Olympia, WA 98504-9162

Street Address:
712 Pear Street SE
Olympia, WA 98504
(360) 586-3162
Fax: (206) 586-3274
(800) 457-6202**

WEST VIRGINIA-
www.state.wv.us

Department of Motor Vehicles:
Department of Motor Vehicles
State Capitol Complex, Bldg 3
Charleston, WV 25317

Drivers License:
Department of Motor Vehicles
800 Washington Street
Charleston, WV 25305

State Archives:
1900 Kanawha Blvd. E
Cultural Center
Capitol Complex
Charleston, WV 25305-0300
(304) 558-0230
Fax: (304) 558-2779
www.wvlc.wvnet.edu/history/
historyw.html

Unclaimed Property:
Office of State Treasurer
Capitol Complex
Charleston, WV 25305
(304) 343-4000

Veteran Affairs Regional Office:
640 Fourth Avenue
Huntington, WV 25701

Vital Records:
Division of Vital Statistics
Capitol Complex, Bldg 3
Room 516
Charleston, WV 25305
(304) 558-2931
(Credit card charges at same
number)
　Marriage: $5 1964- /
　Indexes 1921-1963
　Divorce: County / Indexes
　1967-
　Birth: $5 1917- (some
　1800-1917)
　Death: $5 1917- (some
　1800-1917)

Office of Child Support
Enforcement:
  Department of Health &
  Human Resources
  1900 Kanawha Boulevard East
  Capitol Complex, Bldg 6
  Room 817
  Charleston, WV 25305
  (304) 558-3780
  (800)-249-3778**

WISCONSIN-
www.state.wi.us/agencies/wilis/

Department of Motor Vehicles:
  Registration Files
  Wisconsin Department. of
  Transportation
  PO Box 7909
  Madison, WI 53707

Drivers License:
  Department of Transportation
  PO Box 7918
  Madison, WI 53707-7995
  (608) 264-2353
  (609) 267-3636

State Archives:
  816 State Street
  Madison, WI 53706
  (608) 264-6400
  Fax: (608) 264-6577
  www.dpl.state.wi.us/dicl/
  www.wisc.edu/shs-archives

Unclaimed Property:
  State Treasurer s Office
  PO Box 2114
  Madison, WI 53701-2114
  (608) 267-7977
  www.unclaimed.org

Veteran Affairs Regional Office:
  5000 W National Ave
  Bldg 6
  Milwaukee, WI 53295-4000

Vital Records:
  Section of Vital Statistics
  PO Box 309
  Madison, WI 53701
  266-1371 / (608) 266-1372
    Marriage: $7 1870-
    Divorce: $7 1907-
    Birth: $12 1870-
    Death: $7 1870-

Office of Child Support
Enforcement:
  Division of Economic Support
  PO Box 7935
  Madison, WI 53707-7935

Street Address:
  201 E Washington Avenue
  Room 271
  Madison, WI 53707
  (608) 266-9909
  Fax: (608) 267-2824

WYOMING-www.state.wy.us

Department of Motor Vehicles:
  Department of Revenue
  Motor Vehicle Division
  122 W Twenty-fifth Street
  Cheyenne, WY 82202

Drivers License:
  Department of Revenue
  122 W Twenty-fifth Street
  Cheyenne, WY 82002

State Archives:
  6101 Yellowstone Road
  Cheyenne, WY 82002
  (307) 777-7827
  Fax: (307) 777-7044
www.wsl.state.wy.us/

Unclaimed Property:
  State Treasurer's Office
  1st Floor W. Herschler Bldg
  122 W Twenty-fifth Street
  Cheyenne, WY 82002
  (307) 777-5590
www.state.wyus/state/government/
stat-agencies/treasurer.html

Vital Records:
  Division of Vital Records
  Hathaway Bldg
  Cheyenne, WY 82002
  (307) 777-7591
    Marriage: $12 1941-
    Divorce: $12 1941-
    Birth: $12 1909-
    Death: $9 1909-
www.state.wy.us

Office of Child Support
Enforcement:
  Department of Family
  Services
  2300 Capital Avenue,
  3rd Floor
  Cheyenne, WY 82002-0490
  (307) 777-6948
  Fax: (307) 777-3693

*In-State Only   **Nationwide

Social Security Numbers

The first three numbers in a Social Security number tell you where the card was originally applied for:

001–003	New Hampshire	429–432	Arkansas
004–007	Maine	433–439	Louisiana
008–009	Vermont	440–448	Oklahoma
010–034	Massachusetts	449–467	Texas
035–039	Rhode Island	468–477	Minnesota
040–049	Connecticut	478–485	Iowa
050–134	New York	486–500	Missouri
135–158	New Jersey	501–502	North Dakota
159–211	Pennsylvania	503–504	South Dakota
212–220	Maryland	505–508	Nebraska
221–222	Delaware	509–515	Kansas
223–231	Virginia	516–517	Montana
232–236	West Virginia	518–519	Idaho
237–246	North Carolina	520	Wyoming
247–251	South Carolina	521–524	Colorado
252–260	Georgia	525	New Mexico
261–267	Florida	526–527	Arizona
268–302	Ohio	528–529	Utah
303–317	Indiana	530	Nevada
318–361	Illinois	531–539	Washington
362–386	Michigan	540–544	Oregon
387–399	Wisconsin	545–573	California
400–407	Kentucky	574	Alasaka
409–415	Tennessee	575–576	Hawaii
416–424	Alabama	577–579	Washington, DC
425–428	Mississippi		

Suggested Readings

Anonymous. *How to Create a New Identity*. New York: Citadel, 1983.

Asking, Hane, and Bob Oskarn. *Search*. New York: Harper & Row, 1982.

Carden, Caroline, et al, *Caroline and Just Me*. Fort Worth: Harvest Media, Inc., 1997.

Culligan, Joseph J. *You, Too, Can Find Anybody*. North Miami, FL: Hallmark, 1991.

———*When in Doubt, Check Him Out*. North Miami, FL: Hallmark, 1993.

Doane, Gilbert H., and James R. Dell. *Searching for Your Ancestors*. Fifth Ed. Minneapolis: University of Minnesota Press, 1990.

Faron, Fay. *A Nasty Bit of Business*. San Francisco: Creighton-Morgan, 1988.

French, Scott. *The Big Brother Game*. Secaucus, NJ: Lyle Stuart, 1975.

Hauser, Greg. *So You Wanna Be a P.I., Huh Binky?* Lowell, MI: Hauser & Assoc. 1992.

Jacobson, Trudy, and Gary McClain. *State of the Art Fact-Finding*. New York: Dell. 1993.

King, Dennis. *Get the Facts on Anyone*. New York: Prentice-Hall, 1992.

Klunder, Virgil, and Troy Dunn. *The Locator*. Klunder & Dunn. 1992.

Johnson, Richard. *How to Locate Anyone Who Is or Has Been in the Military*. Fifth Ed. San Antonio: MIE, 1993.

Johnson, Richard. *The Abandoned Money Book*. San Antonio: MIE, 1992.

Lapin, Lee. *How to Get Anything on Anybody Book*. San Mateo, CA: ISECO, 1991.

Pankau, Ed. *Check It Out*. Chicago: Contemporary, 1992.

Rothfeder, Jeffrey. *Privacy for Sale*. New York: Simon & Schuster, 1992.

Sullivan, Charlene, and Robert Johnson. *Credit and Collections for Small Stores*. Washington, DC: U.S. Small Business Administration.

Thomas, Ralph. *Advanced Skip Tracing Techniques*. New York: Thomas, 1989.

Tillman, Norma. *The Adoption Searcher's Handbook,* rev. ed. Nashville, TN: Norma Tillman Enterprises, 1997.

———*The Man with the Turquoise Eyes and Other True Stories of a Private Eye's Search for Missing Persons*. Nashville: Rutledge Hill Press, 1995.

www.reunion.com—ORDER FORM
(Prices subject to change. All prices are as of 1998)

Date:_____   Amount enclosed: _____

Name: _____

Address:_____

City: _____St:_____ Zip:_____ Country:_____

Phone: _____

Method of payment: Check   Money Order   Visa   MasterCard
(Please make payable to Norma Tillman)

Credit card: _____ Exp. Date:_____

Signature of card holder:_____

Please check what you wish to order:
- ☐ **Missing Persons Registry**—www.reunion.com—$20.00 (per year)
- ☐ **Missing Persons Magazine Classified Ad**—www.reunion.com—$20.00 (per year)
- ☐ **Missing Persons Magazine Subscription**—www.reunion.com—$25.00 (quarterly)
- ☐ The **Adoption Searcher's Handbook**—$21.95 (includes s&h)

  Nationwide Locating Service—www.nationwidelocate.com

  Information Broker Services:
- ☐   Surname search: $ 50.00
- ☐   Name, date of birth: $100.00
- ☐   First name, date of birth $150.00
- ☐   Social Security number traced: $250.00
- ☐   Death record: $ 30.00
- ☐   Phone number: $ 50.00
- ☐   Address verification: $ 50.00
- ☐   Neighbors of last known address: $ 25.00
- ☐   Guaranteed locate: $500.00

  (You provide correct name; date of birth; social security number; and if possible a last known address and we'll find this person in 60 days or less or refund your money. Certain restrictions apply: Missing persons must be over 18 years of age and not wanted by law-enforcement or for collection purposes; must be in U.S.; must be a relative or friend only.)

Missing Person Information:

What is the reason for the separation from this person? Adoption/Divorce/Lost contact/
Moved/Other

Is the missing person adopted?   Y   N   Are you adopted?   Y   N

Name: _____

Date of birth: _____ Age:_____ Place of birth: _____

Social Security Number: _____

Lask known address: _____

Other identifying information:_____

If adopted: Place of adoption: _____Hospital of birth:_____

Other adoption information: _____

Classified ad: (You attach a separate page for this.) _____

Circle type of missing person: Abandoned; Adoption; Classmate: Family; First Love; Friend;
Heir; Military

Norma Tillman Enterprises/P.O. Box 290333/Nashville, TN 37229-0333/www.reunion.com